HOPIS, TEWAS,
AND THE AMERICAN ROAD

EDITED BY WILLARD WALKER AND LYDIA L. WYCKOFF

UNIVERSITY OF NEW MEXICO PRESS, ALBUQUERQUE

Library of Congress Cataloging-in-Publication Data

Hopis, Tewas, and the American road.

  Reprint. Originally published: Middletown, Conn.:
Wesleyan University, 1983.
  Bibliography: p.
  1. Hopi Indians. 2. Tewa Indians. 3. Hopi
Indians—Art. 4. Tewa Indians—Art. 5. Melville,
Carey E., 1978– —Art collections. 6. Melville,
Maud Seamen, 1880– —Art collections. 7. Indians
of North America—Southwest, New—Art. I. Walker,
Willard. II. Wyckoff, Lydia L.
E99.H7H695   1986   738.3'7   86-7078
ISBN 0-8263-0918-6
ISBN 0-8263-0919-4 (pbk.)

Then hear thou in heaven, and forgive the sin of thy servants, and of thy people Israel, that thou teach them the good way wherein they should walk, and give rain upon thy land, which thou hast given to thy people for an inheritance.

The Book of Kings 8:36

CONTENTS

Rio Grande Tewa
Navajo & Pima
Plains & Plateau Peoples

ILLUSTRATIONS

Professor and Mrs. Carey E. Melville—1929

ACKNOWLEDGMENTS

We are much indebted to the descendants of the Melvilles for their aid in facilitating Wesleyan's acquisition of the Melville Collection and for their consistent support of this project. Maud Melville Arnold, Martha Melville Fletcher and Robert Seaman Melville have all searched their memories and attics to make the account of their trip to the Southwest as accurate as possible. Robert S. Arnold of Sturbridge, Massachusetts, has also given of his time and talent, printing the photographs included in this text from his grandfather's negatives.

In spite of the Melvilles' carefully preserved documentation and the memories of their children, information was still lacking. Gaps in the record have been filled by the members of the First Mesa Baptist Church in Polacca. This book has benefited substantially from the kind cooperation and encouragement of Reverend Roger Ramsel of Polacca. To him and the members of the Baptist Church we express our sincere thanks.

As memory has served such an important role in the preparation of this volume, it is most fortunate that it could be researched and written now, while there are still people who remember the 1920s at Hopi. Research and publication of this book were made possible by generous gifts from the following Wesleyan alumni and their families: Mrs. Jule H. Coffey, Mrs. Edward L. Lloyd, Katharine L. McKenna, Dr. Malcolm C. McKenna, Mr. Donald C. McKenna, and others who wish to remain anonymous. These gifts were supplemented by the generosity of Mr. David P. Usher, President, The Greenwich Workshop. We thank them all for helping to make this book a reality.

We should also like to express our thanks to the institutions and private collectors who aided us in our research. These are: The American Museum of Natural History; the Clark University Archives; Hurst and Hurst Gallery; the Indian Law Resource Center, The Museum of the American Indian, Heye Foundation; The Museum of Northern Arizona; The Peabody Museum, Harvard University; Mr. Julius Gold and Mr. Bruce Green.

Wesleyan University has, from the beginning, provided support and guidance. Many individuals have assisted in our undertaking; we would particularly like to express our gratitude to Gwynthlyn Green, Valborg L. Proudman and Edwina Ranganathan of the Anthropology Department, Annie V. F. Storr of the Center for the Arts, William H. Van Saun of the Office of Public Information and Publications, and Robert L. Kirkpatrick of the Office of University Relations.

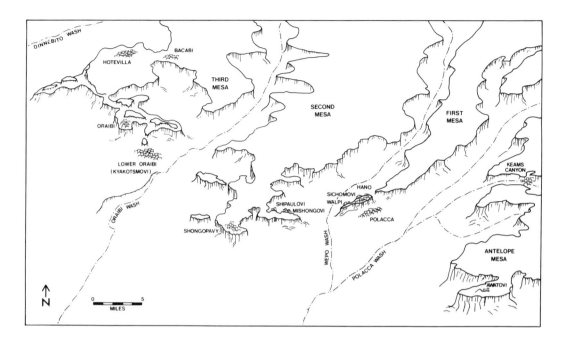

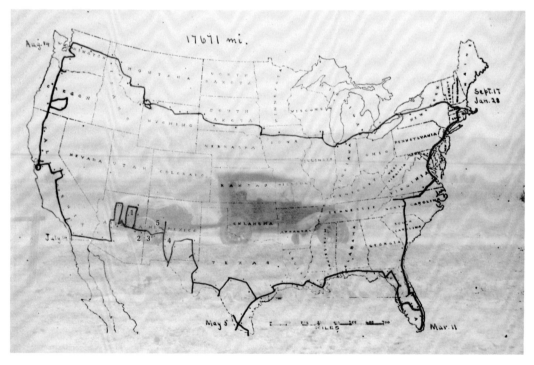

On the Road with the Melvilles—Route of the 1927 trip and a detailed map of the Hopi mesas
(1. Hopi, 2. Zuni, 3. Acoma-Laguna, 4. Isleta, 5. Rio Grande Tewa—San Juan, Santa Clara and
San Ildefonso)

CHAPTER 1

INTRODUCTION

The evidence of archaeology and of Indian oral tradition indicates that the ancestors of the Hopi Indians have lived for some nine centuries in stone masonry villages in the same general area of northern Arizona (Jennings 1974: 303). Another similar village on First Mesa has been occupied by Tewa Indians since the beginning of the eighteenth century. (See map, opposite page.) The desert environment and the remote location, far from the major river valleys and transportation routes of America, have shielded these people from some of the more traumatic consequences of both the Spanish and Anglo American conquests of the Southwest. They have not been entirely unmolested, however.

The art form which is commonly identified with the Hopis, despite the fact that it has always been exclusively associated with the Tewas and the Hopis of First Mesa, is a product of the interaction of social, cultural and economic factors which have been at work in the Hopi area over the past century. The Melville Collection of Indian art, which was donated to Wesleyan University by Mrs. Carey E. Melville of Worcester, Massachusetts, in 1976, reflects much of the social and cultural ferment that has attended the confrontation of Hopi, Tewa, and American societies and values during this period. And an understanding of the social, economic, and political history of this area can shed considerable light on the items in the collection. In what follows we hope to provide the information and perspectives necessary to interpret the collection and to appreciate it, not simply as an array of beautiful Indian antiques, but as a native Indian record of three-way cultural contact and change.

The collection, or most of it, was made in a three-week period in 1927 by an American family from Massachusetts who set off on a trip around America in their Model T Ford without any intention of making an extended visit to the Hopi Reservation. The Hopi-Tewa items, and the Melvilles' extensive and meticulous documentation of many of these items, on film as well as on paper, make the collection unusually informative. It includes a wide range of ceramic items produced on the Hopi Mesas in 1927. These include traditional pieces for local use, innovative items for sale to tourists, and ceramics that illustrate the broad range of experimentation and development during an extremely complex and poorly understood period in the long history of Hopi pottery—the time of transition from folk craft to "Indian Art."

Hopi ceramics are part of a tradition that can be traced back for more than 15 centuries (Jennings 1974: 303), a tradition that became particularly well known during the late nineteenth and early twentieth centuries. Any interpretation of the Melville Collection can benefit from the Keam Collection of the late nineteenth century, which is now on tour around the United States. A catalogue of this collection has recently been published (Wade and McChesney 1980). An analysis of the emergence of "art pottery" as "big business" on First Mesa can also rely on the earlier scholarship of Ruth Bunzel in the 1920s, the Coltons in the 1930s, Edward P. Dozier in the 1950s, Kathryn Sikorski in the 1960s, and Michael Stanislawski in the 1970s. But some of the keys that will be crucial in unraveling the history of the Hopi art form can be provided only by the Melville Collection, for this collection and its documentation provide crucial information as to who was making what, when, and where.

Mrs. Melville gave her collection to Wesleyan University at the suggestion of her grandson, Robert S. Arnold, who had graduated from Wesleyan in 1969 and had studied with Willard Walker in the Anthropology Department. The collection has been stored in the department since 1976, where portions of it have been displayed from time to time.

Lea S. McChesney graduated from Bard College in 1976, where she wrote a thesis called "Navajo weaving: symbol of a contemporary nativistic process." She received her M.A. in anthropology from Wesleyan in 1978, where she wrote a thesis on "Man as meaning-seeker, mediator, and master: a comparative analysis of Hopi, Zuni, and Navajo symbolic systems." She also received the Frank Hamilton Cushing Award for the best student paper in anthropology at Wesleyan that year. In 1979 she became a Curatorial Associate at the Peabody Museum of Archaeology and Ethnology at Harvard University, where she now serves as Director of the Hemenway-Keam Research Project. She is the co-author, with Edwin L. Wade, of *Historic Hopi Ceramics: The Thomas V. Keam Collection of the Peabody Museum of Archaeology and Ethnology*, Harvard University, published by the Peabody Museum Press in 1981. She is also the author of a *Reference Manual for Historic Hopi Ceramics* (1982). Her work on the Keam Collection has informed her analysis of the Melville Collection, which is comparable in many respects, as she points out in "On the Road with the Melvilles," chapter 2 of this volume. Ms. McChesney's chapter describes the people who made the collection, their objectives, attitudes, and perceptions, and the unusual amount of written and photographic documentation which they provided for most of the items they collected. And it gives a series of intimate glimpses into Mrs. Melville's diary and Ethel Salyah's correspondence which reveal many of the concerns and aspirations of the Hopis and Tewas of First Mesa at the time when they were transforming an ancient craft into a modern art form.

In 1978–'79 Katharine L. McKenna acted as curator of the collection at Wesleyan and catalogued it for the university before graduating *cum laude* in American studies with a concentration in anthropology. After her graduation she became a museum assistant at the Museum of Northern Arizona where she had occasion to assist in the organization, production, inventory, and installation of various exhibits sponsored by the museum including the annual Hopi and Navajo "Shows." She was also responsible for collecting and returning items from the Hopi and Navajo reservations, supervising the judging, and photodocumenting the prizewinning pieces. Her essay on "Art, business and the American road", Chapter 3 of this volume, uses the knowledge and experience which she acquired in this position to give a sense of how the Indian art business works. It also shows how criteria of excellence have been established and maintained and how it is that judges, dealers, tourists and Indian artists, despite their disagreements on the relative merits of specific items, manage nonetheless to achieve a rough consensus on the overall standards of excellence that apply to Southwestern Indian art.

Robert E. Cleaves, like all the others, studied with Willard Walker in the Anthropology Department before writing a senior thesis which enabled him to graduate from Wesleyan with the class of '82 and with honors in general scholarship. This thesis, which was called "A White man's government: the Hopi, the Northern Cheyenne, and the Indian Reorganization Act of 1934," placed considerable emphasis on the effects on the Hopi Reservation of the Indian Reorganization Act and thus provided much of the background for Mr. Cleaves' "The American road to freedom and enlightenment," Chapter 4 of this volume. In this chapter Mr. Cleaves sketches the history of the Christian missions on the Hopi Reservation over the past century and the tortuous path of federal Indian policy during the same period. This is intended as a description of the historical and political context in which the Hopis and Tewas developed their ceramic art in the 1920s and 1930s.

Chapter 5, "The Hopis and the Tewas," was written by Willard Walker on the basis of materials previously published, particularly those by the late Edward P. Dozier and by Michael B. Stanislawski. Mr. Walker has taught anthropology at Wesleyan since 1966 and did field research in the Southwest prior to that date, though never in the Hopi area. His chapter attempts to describe the relationships between the Hopis and the Tewas, the mechanisms by which the ethnic boundary between these two groups has been maintained, despite intermarriage and acculturation, and the methods by which the Tewa minority has sought to overcome the prejudice of the Hopi majority.

Lydia L. Wyckoff earned the M.A. in anthropology at Wesleyan in 1976. She has done archaeological fieldwork in Nicaragua and, more recently, ethnoarchaeological and sociocultural research at Zuni (1979) and on the Hopi Mesas (1979–1980). Her Ph.D. dissertation on "Third Mesa Hopi ceramics: a study of the ceramic domain" is expected to take final form in 1983. It has already served as the basis for much of the data and analysis in "The Sikyatki Revival," Chapter 6 of this volume. In this chapter Ms. Wyckoff analyzes the Hopi-Tewa pottery and defines a number of wares. These form a chronological sequence which she attempts to account for in terms of the social, cultural, political, and economic factors that are more fully discussed in previous chapters. She concludes that, although Sikyatki Revival Style wares are a radical departure from the pottery produced in the nineteenth century, they are also an expression of cultural continuity.

The catalogue section of this volume presents Ms. Wyckoff's analysis of the materials in the collection other than Hopi-Tewa pottery.

As a whole, the volume attempts to present a series of accounts of Hopi-Tewa-American relations, with particular emphasis on the 1920s and 1930s and on the emergence and crystalization of the art of the "Sikyatki Revival."

But we approach this art from several perspectives—that of the tourist-collectors, that of the Indian art judges, critics, curators, and dealers, and from a consideration of the art, itself, treated as a set of native documents which change through time and thus are indices of circumstance as perceived by their makers. And since no art form exists but in a social, cultural, economic, and political context, we attempt to reconstruct some of the broad outlines of this context as it may have existed in the 1920s and 1930s. And, if our efforts are not entirely successful, we rely on the photographs scattered through this book to paint the scene.

CHAPTER 2

ON THE ROAD WITH THE MELVILLES

THE COLLECTION

The Melville Collection consists of 181 objects of Plains, Pueblo, Pima, and Navajo origin together with photographs, correspondence, and other documentation. Most of the 181 were obtained in 1927 by Professor and Mrs. Carey E. Melville in the Hopi region, particularly at the village of Polacca, at the foot of First Mesa. Of these Hopi pieces, 86 are ceramic; and these are the subject of a detailed analysis in Chapter 6. The Plains material, which dates from the late nineteenth century, originally belonged to Mrs. Melville's father, who was a Methodist minister in the midwest. According to Martha Fletcher, the youngest Melville daughter, Mrs. Melville's father acquired this material from missionaries. Perhaps this childhood association with American Indian art gave Mrs. Melville the initial interest which later generated her enthusiasm for items of Hopi manufacture. But even if we cannot state this with any certainty, we do know that Maud Melville appreciated a variety of articles made by American Indians.

The Melville Collection is not limited to objects that are normally considered American Indian art, since it contains such prosaic items as drills, corncobs, and *piki* bread. The Hopi material includes a wide, though not exhaustive, sample of artifacts made and used in the Hopi villages in the 1920s; it is, and was intended as, a small material culture collection. Thus, while the collection does include some pieces that are useful in reconstructing the history of American Indian art, the collection as a whole, and the Hopi material in particular, has considerable ethnographic significance, quite apart from its relevance to Indian art and art history. This ethnographic significance derives from the fact that the collection was made at reasonably well defined places and times and much of it is well documented. This is both unusual and fortuitous, particularly in view of the fact that the collectors were not trained ethnographers. The major portion of the collection was acquired during a cross-country family trip. Because this trip was central to the making of the Melville Collection, this discussion will focus on the trip and the associations it held for the Melvilles.

It is instructive to compare the Melville Collection with certain better known museum collections. The Hopi material, for example is reminiscent of the "Thomas V. Keam Collection of Hopi Material Culture" at the Peabody Museum at Harvard. It differs primarily in scale: the Keam Collection consists of some 4500 pieces. The range of material is quite similar, however. Both collections include ceramics, textiles, baskets, implements, and painted wooden objects. But the Keam Collection, which was made during the last quarter of the nineteenth century, represents an earlier period of Hopi history and comprises many more items. Otherwise it differs from the Melville Collection in only one important respect: it contains far more ceremonial items and ritual paraphernalia, e.g., dance wands, kilts, *tablitas,* and pottery vessels associated with native rituals.

This disparity between the two collections can best be accounted for in terms of the collectors' varying degrees of access to Hopi society and the length of time they spent collecting, as well as the time of their arrival. Keam lived in the vicinity of the Hopi villages for some 25 years, from 1876 to 1902. The Melvilles were in the Hopi area for three weeks, in June 1927. They made brief visits again in 1934 and 1954, although it is very unlikely that they collected many items during these two later visits. Equally important may be the fact that Keam, as a trader, had many long-term Hopi acquaintances in a period before Federal agents and Protestant Missionaries exerted any great degree of power or influence on the Hopi Mesas. The Melvilles, on the other hand, were guests of Baptist missionaries, one of whom was a family friend; and it was through these Baptists, who relentlessly opposed the native priesthoods, that they made their contacts. This accounts for the fact that items associated with the native religion are not well represented in the Melville Collection. (Those that are, a single prayer-stick and some of the rattles, have no prayer plumes attached.) As guests of the Baptist missionaries, the Melvilles felt constrained to attend Christian services exclusively and, hence, did not attend any of the native religious ceremonies.

Since the Melville Collection was intended as a material culture collection and not as a collection of American Indian art, it is not confined to expensive or aesthetically outstanding pieces. It does include some unusual pieces which document the developmental years of the American Indian art market in the Southwest. The two examples of Black on Black pottery made by Maria Martinez of San Ildefonso Pueblo are good examples. Their polished surfaces lack the gunmetal quality which Maria eventually achieved and which came to be her trademark. Although in 1927 she was not the widely known and renowned potter that she was later to become, her reputation was sufficiently established that Mrs. Melville thought it important to have some examples of her work. These pieces would not be considered Maria Martinez masterpieces, but they are valuable because they shed light on a stage in the development of an art form. Maud Melville did not purchase them for their monetary value, according to her son, Dr. Robert Melville, but because she thought they were notable and unique.

Maria's reputation as a Southwestern potter is rivaled only by Nampeyo, a Tewa woman from First Mesa. Nampeyo was already famous when the Melvilles arrived in 1927. By this time, however, she was at an advanced age and, though she still made pots, she could no longer decorate them, due to failing eyesight. Like all the traditional Indian potters, Nampeyo may never have signed her pottery. Her daughters carried on the tradition; but, under the influence of Anglo traders, who thought it advantageous to identify the work of specific individuals, they began to sign their products.

The Melville collection is by no means confined to pottery, as we have already noted. If ceramics are particularly well represented, this is probably due to Mrs. Melville's love of china and ceramics. But the chief value of the collection does not lie either in the individual pieces or in its breadth. Rather, the value lies in the accompanying documentation, which provides a human context and an added dimension for the collection. Like other collectors, the Melvilles were motivated by aesthetic considerations in making purchases. In some instances, as Robert Melville recalls, they collected because the objects were the color of the earth. But like ethnographers, and unlike art collectors, they were sensitive to the social context from which their acquisitions derived, as well as to the social and cultural contexts in which they were acquired.

In fact, the Melvilles did not originally set out to collect pottery or even Indian art. They simply embarked on a family camping trip around America in their Model T Ford. The collection was an afterthought, one of the things they did on the trip, like taking photographs and keeping a diary, to record, extend, and define their experience. They discovered, quite adventitiously it seems, an "exotic" people who made beautiful objects, some of which they brought back to Worcester, Massachusetts. One of the more interesting aspects of the collection is that, with its accompanying documentation, it records the story of an American family who set out to explore America and discovered that its social and cultural dimensions match the scenic attractions of its geography.

It is, then, not only the Melville Collection that is being presented here. Never simply a collection of objects, it is accompanied by ample, varied, and rich documentation, a rare occurrence indeed. The documentation and the collection together constitute a marvelous and peculiarly American story of adventure, exploration, and cultural exchange. It is this story which has captured my own interest, because it provides a human context in which to view the objects. Thanks to the documentation, the story can be told largely in the words of those who lived it: Mrs. Maud Melville kept a diary during the family trip on which they began actively collecting, and in later years she wrote extensive notes for lectures on such diverse topics as the trip itself, Hopi life and customs, and the music of the Southwestern Indians. These lectures were illustrated with lantern slides taken by her husband; so this is Professor Melville's story as well. And then there is the story of life on the Hopi Mesas as told to Mrs. Melville by the Baptist missionaries at Polacca, who hosted the Melville family during their stay, and by Ethel Salyah of Polacca, who corresponded faithfully with Mrs. Melville for over ten years thereafter. Her poignant story of the hardships of Hopi life in the late 1920s and 1930s is phrased in a naive, awkward English which is, nonetheless, the universal language of human experience.

Since making the collection was but one facet of a much larger event, a family trip around America, and the trip was but a small segment—barely nine months—in the lives of a remarkable family, we must ask who these people were and what the nature of their experience may have been.

THE COLLECTORS

Maud Seamen met Carey E. Melville in 1900, while both were students at Northwestern University. She was majoring in philosophy, studying the psychological impact of advertising on the public; he was majoring in philosophy also, which he combined with Greek and mathematics into a triple major. He graduated Phi Beta Kappa from Northwestern in 1901, after which he attended Johns Hopkins University for a year of graduate study, followed by a year's teaching fellowship at what is now Case Western Reserve. She graduated from Northwestern in 1903; a year later they were married.

Torn between a life in the ministry and a teaching profession, Carey Melville chose the latter since, as his daughter Maud Arnold, recalls, he was a religious man but not "in the church sense." He faced another important choice soon after his marriage and the decision to pursue teaching: whether to accept a position in California or in Massachusetts. New England was unfamiliar to the young couple. Originally from Maryland and Virginia, Carey Melville's family moved to Chicago when he was 14. He was the eldest of ten children, born in 1878. Maud Seamen was born in La Prairie Centre, Illinois in 1880, the eldest of three girls. Her father was a Methodist minister who emigrated from England at the age of two. During her youth in central Illinois, her family had often moved from parish to parish. The decision to move to New England was made on the basis of a desire "to be at the scene of so much early history."

So, in 1906, Carey Melville joined the faculty of Clark University as Honorary Fellow in Mathematics. Clark was a newly founded and unique institution of higher learning, oriented exclusively toward the sciences. The lines between students and faculty were almost indistinct; and Honorary Fellows, because they were intermediate between the two, in fact erased any distinction. The top men of their fields were at Clark during Carey Melville's early years there, and it was an intimate environment with a highly charged intellectual atmosphere of quality teaching and research in the sciences.

Carey Melville was an exacting teacher; he was also devoted to a solid preparation in general education. In addition to his teaching position, which he held until 1948, he served as University Registrar for eighteen years (1914–1932). As Registrar, he designed a broad, demanding curriculum in liberal arts education which might at first glance appear inappropriate to an institution with strong emphasis on graduate research in the sciences. But Professor Melville was devoted to teaching, not research, and his philosophy of education stressed what he called "general cultural values" (Melville Papers, Clark University Archives).

Professor Melville was a good father and remembered his children with "little unexpected treats and surprises." According to Maud Arnold, "after the midday meal, he would read aloud to us for an hour or so before walking back to the college." The responsibility to be a contributing member of a working community was communicated to children and students alike.

Maud Melville shared these basic beliefs with her husband. Her public activities and interests were many, and she was "a great person for organizations," serving as President of the Worcester Women's Club, the College Club (which subsequently became the American Association of University Women), and the Clark University Faculty Women's Club. Like her husband, she was devoted to scholarship, and she assisted the Worcester Philharmonic in its efforts to raise scholarship money for young students. She also lectured at the Massachusetts Indian Association in support of scholarship money for Indian youth. It was not until she reached the age of 90 that her activities became restricted, and then only by a broken hip. Maud Melville lectured "with camera and trailer" across western Massachusetts, primarily to church and youth organizations, for nearly ten years after the trip. Both Carey and Maud Melville were extremely gifted individuals. He was known as a "Renaissance Man;" she was "kind of a dreamer."

THE JOURNEY

When, at 49, Professor Melville was given a sabbatical leave from Clark, it was decided that the entire family, including three children, aged 15, 13, and 9, would set out to tour the country. "Bounding the United States," Mrs. Melville called it. After Christmas vacation in 1926, the children did not go back to school, and on January 29, 1927, the family of five—Professor and Mrs. Melville, Maud, Robert, and Martha—set out from Worcester in their new 1927 Model T Ford, named "Hubbub," and headed south.

This was no ordinary trip. The Melvilles met with many gloomy predictions both before leaving and all along the way: the Ford would *never* make it; they were going into the wilds with "rattlers, Indians, bandits"; how could the children miss school? why didn't they go abroad? That was the more civilized thing to do; and camping was a disreputable way to travel.

But they were ready for anything, and they had answers to everyone's questions. As a student of geology, Professor Melville wanted to see the great wonders of the western landscape, Santa Elena Canyon in particular. The trip was to last for nine months, so the children would be back in time to reenter school in the fall. Their grades were sufficiently good that to miss a few months wouldn't matter; and the education they would receive through the trip would be much broader than any they might have in school. "Hubbub" was equipped with a special power drive for getting out of trouble; and, after all, Professor Melville was an expert navigator and mechanic.

Maud Arnold remembers that her parents were "used to adapting to life" and "making the best of difficulty." The entire group was "self-contained, pretty much, as long as the car went." Carefully selected camping equipment had already been purchased and shipped south, out of the snowbelt, to Carey Melville's brother in North Carolina, where it was subsequently picked up. From that point on, everything was hauled behind them in a trailer: spare car parts, camera equipment, food, cooking utensils, "a great big old udder of a canvas water bag," and Mrs. Melville's handmade sleeping bags. "Hubbub" was even equipped with a "Thef-a-larm," should they meet any highwaymen along the way. They had traveled little before this; but they believed in "seeing America first."

In all, the Melvilles covered 17,671 miles in just under nine months. During the 231 days on the road, 128 stops were made with the following overnight accommodations: 83 "tent ups," 16 visits with friends, 6 tourist rooms, 5 "skies," 4 camps, 3 hotels, and 1 adobe house. Delays due to inclement weather were made because of rains in North Carolina, Florida, and Texas, and mud in New Mexico. Car problems also caused delays, and Mrs. Melville noted the following in her itinerary: radiator leak in Texas (20 minutes), accelerator problem in New Mexico (30 minutes), gas strainer in California (30 minutes), and spark plugs in Montana (30 minutes). In all, she recorded less than two hours' delay for automotive problems. But Robert Melville, who assisted his father with mechanical repairs, recalls that there were some more substantial difficulties: an overnight delay in Grants, New Mexico to regrind the valves, and the installation of new piston rings in San Francisco. This also caused an overnight delay, but the Melvilles were visiting family, so it was not a great inconvenience.

The longest day's drive was 321 miles; the shortest, 6; the average was 200. The trailer was unloaded on a one-way road into the Grand Canyon National Park when, despite its special power drive, "Hubbub" could not pull the loaded trailer up a 20 degree grade on a gravel road; the combined weight of car and trailer, packed, was 4,000 pounds! Driving a rectangular route across the continental United States, the Melvilles crossed the border into Mexico five times and into Canada twice. Only one accident occurred on the trip: near Joliet, Illinois, the car fishtailed in a rainstorm and knocked the trailer off its axle.

Passing the Hopi Buttes on the road to Polacca—1927

All along the route Mrs. Melville kept her diary and an itinerary. She noted people as well as scenery, especially their reception by strangers and the recognition they received from fellow out-of-staters or those who had themselves visited Massachusetts. In Santa Fe, they saw 30 different car licenses. Contrasts between regions were recorded in details of landscape, cuisine, and dialect; she even noted the price of meals in restaurants, listing the prices of everything on the menu. The condition of roads, and the availability of bath, shower, and laundry facilities were duly noted. The further west they went, the higher the thermometer climbed; this too was duly noted.

Before arriving at the Hopi Mesas, they visited New Mexico, where they crossed the Mescalero Apache reservation near White Sands National Monument, and where they visited Isleta and Laguna Pueblos. At this point Mrs. Melville's entries grow longer; her jotted notes become a rich prose.

Their three-week stay at Polacca (illustration page 43) as guests of missionary friends, the "Misses Humes and Ryan," was a welcome change of pace from the rest of the trip. Although they still managed to travel a great deal, stopping at nearly every village on the three mesas, they had an opportunity to enjoy the generosity of their friends and to observe a life style which was quite different from their own. The Melville children played with Hopi children and rode horses through the mesa country. Mrs. Melville watched Hopi women at work cooking and making pottery and baskets; she and the children even had a lesson in pottery making. This was a way of entering into Hopi life. To have this brief but intimate association with Hopis was a rare privilege for all.

COLLECTING THE MELVILLE WAY

The Melvilles would, no doubt, have endorsed the sentiments of Erna Fergusson's dedication in *Dancing Gods* (1931), a book which Carey Melville gave his wife for Christmas in 1932:

> Southwestern Indians have no better friends than artists, who recognize that the Indian is essentially an artist. They value his art in all its forms, they help him without condescension, and they respect his integrity too much to try to make him over into something foreign.

The Melvilles did not acquire artifacts as a kind of investment as is often done today. Nor were they motivated by scientific concerns, as was their predecessor, Thomas V. Keam, who had commissioned potters to make reproductions of types of pottery which had not been made for generations, so that a complete sample of historic and proto-historic Hopi wares could be included in the collections he assembled for research museums (Wade and McChesney 1980:9). Both Professor and Mrs. Melville wanted to collect material that best represented the life they observed while guests at Polacca.

Yet the Melvilles also collected, like most other collectors, on the basis of aesthetic considerations. With regard to the ceramics in the collection, this meant a consideration of the quality of the shape of the vessel and its surface finish, the fineness of the line work, if painted, or its lustre, if polished. According to Maud Arnold, her parents "bought by line and design. They had a sense . . . of what was beautiful."

This shared aesthetic sense was wide ranging and stemmed from an individual artistic aptitude in each. Professor Melville was an accomplished amateur photographer who exhibited internationally. Mrs. Melville was a weaver and made enamelled and hammered copper plates with free form, contemporary designs. She especially appreciated items made by hand and had a strong desire to understand their manufacture. The diversity and ecclecticism of their tastes is reflected not only in the range of American Indian material they collected but also in the fact that American Indian material was not all they collected. According to Maud Arnold,

> They just collected, period. Everything. I have bags and boxes of geological specimens and fossils. Rocks everywhere! And they collected Japanese art, books and prints. They were marvelous archivists . . .

They kept old letters and made a point of documenting their acquisitions, especially their American Indian items. Mrs. Melville was particularly fond of family-related materials; and the "generations of cookbooks" she passed on to her daughter included one from her great-grandmother.

The Melville aesthetic was rooted in a desire to preserve and record, to somehow capture an experience, and if this experience had any human element it was all the more imperative that it be preserved. Knowing about the potters, the designs, and the way Hopi pots were made was as exciting as the pieces themselves. Hence Mrs. Melville was particularly concerned with keeping tabs on where a pot came from. The Melvilles, therefore, were preservers and conservators of knowledge as well as collectors of what they considered beautiful.

Professor and Mrs. Melville "made an art out of living," according to their daughter; and their capacity to enjoy life enabled them to ignore the constraints of time. Thus, at Hopi a brief stop-over was transformed into a timeless treasure. Maud Melville wrote in a letter to her family on June 24, 1927:

> Never in my life have I been in such a place. The thrills we have every hour can't be put in a letter. I'll tell you when I come.
>
> First, if this letter isn't done you'll know Miss Johnson has called, that the postman is here and the mailbag must be closed.
>
> Yesterday we went to see a Hopi woman make a basket. It's perfectly huge—135" circumference and 60" high. She's been offered $300–for it. They have to take down the door to get it out of the house.
>
> Last night we went to the house of one of the Indian Agents and had a wonderful visit. Today we came to this Indian village of basketmakers. This afternoon late I'm going to visit Ethel, an Indian woman who is going to let me try to make a vase. Tomorrow there is to be an Indian wedding in the church. . . .
>
> I know everyday makes us later, but how can we leave when such a rare

opportunity is ours? We are the most fortunate people on earth, I believe. Everyone does wonderful things for us. I wonder if God hasn't a hand in guiding it all. The weather, even, is with us. . . .

On their return to Worcester, the Melvilles had, not only a small but relatively complete material culture collection, but also a collection of photographs and Mrs. Melville's meticulously detailed diary. Further, to keep the experience vivid in their memories, as well as to allow it to continue in their lives, Mrs. Melville corresponded with their missionary hosts, especially Miss Ryan, and with Ethel Salyah and Ruth Takala, two residents of Polacca. She continued to purchase pottery, baskets, textiles, and jewelry through the mail; and she gathered her notes together and researched for background information which she combined with her husband's lantern slides to create a lecture series through which she communicated the family's precious experience to others.

The major portion of the collection was acquired by the Melvilles during the 1927 family trip or in the years immediately succeeding it. Items purchased during the trip came either directly from the maker or from traders at reservation stores such as Tom Pavatea's store in Polacca and trading posts at the New Mexico pueblos and in Leupp, Arizona. In subsequent years additional pieces were purchased through the Ramah Trading Company near Zuni or through Ethel Ryan, one of the Baptist missionaries who had hosted the Melvilles at Hopi, or direct from Ruth Takala and Ethel Salyah. Buying from the maker was preferred, since it established a sort of bond. But whether a piece came directly from the maker or from a middleman, such as a trader or missionary, the crucial consideration for the Melvilles was the quality of personal contact involved. Purchasing was no mere business transaction, it was social interaction and cultural exchange; the Melvilles were gathering rare and privileged information. This was especially true at Hopi, where the Melvilles felt they were able to partake of so much of Hopi life.

The prices of items received from the Ramah Trading Company or from Miss Ryan were stipulated in the correspondence. The late 'twenties and early 'thirties were a low point in the Indian art market, and the sagging prices are recorded in the correspondence. Ethel Ryan wrote as follows on May 31, 1929:

Dear Mrs. Melville:

At last the basket and pottery are on their way. Ruth made three of the pieces and her little Loretta, aged 5, made five. The Oraibi basket was $2.50.   5 pieces of pottery   @ $.05—.25
       2 pieces   @   .10—.20
       1 piece   @   .15—.15
The total is $3.10 plus .78 postage.

A Ramah Trading Company invoice, dated July 5, 1929 is further evidence. (See page 148.)

The manner of payment in transactions with Hopis is less clearly documented. Mrs. Melville did send money to Ethel Salyah, but she often sent other items which were received as gifts and tokens of friendship. Many items were specifically requested; clothing, yard goods, and candy are most frequently mentioned. The Hopis and the Tewas have a long tradition of gift exchange with trading partners of various other ethnic groups, e.g., Navajos, Havasupais, and visitors from the New Mexico pueblos. The following letter was written by Ethel Salyah (who refers to herself as "Ethel Wilfred," Wilfred being her husband's name) to Maud Melville Arnold in 1934, shortly after the latter's marriage to Alfred S. Arnold. Notice how the letter refers again and again to gifts sent and received in the past and anticipates gifts in the future, thus incorporating the new bride into the Hopi-Tewa economic network and obligating her, in her new status as an adult woman, and no doubt her unsuspecting husband, to a pattern of reciprocal gift exchange, like her parents before her and like generations of Navajo and other trading partners. Ethel Salyah's letter reads, in part, as follows:

Polacca Arizona.
July 18. 1934

Hollow Mrs Alfred. S. Arnold.

I and Wilfred we are very glad to see your picture. that your mother sent it to us. and you are a nice looking lady you are. you have your wedding dresses on. and how do you like you little things. that I send. for your wedding. and your Mother worte me. and she said that. you have a new house. that your. husband was very nice. and Wilfred said I wish we could see then. I wish we could, I said to him. and you dont now this little girl we [got], her neam is Vivian. and she is 2 year old, and next month she will be 3 year old now Augs 9. 1934. you just now the boy and little girl that time you were out here. bother of then were gone we lost then again. [Ethel lost her first 10 children to tuberculosis.] and [now] we have a little [one] again. and she is a happy little girl Vivian. and your mother said that they are coming out here again, so we are watining for then. and they haven come yet. plase talk to your mother. and ask her when they are coming out. and they mush tell us when they will come, and tell her we will make the song out here if we can. and also tell her to bring her old stockings for me. I have been sewing my old stocking all the time. and brign her anther old things, to. well Mrs Maude I am glad for you when you get merring. so be king [kind?] to your man. and be with him all the tine that what I am out here. so I am with my one husband yet. some of the Hopi Indain are not bining withe there ones [own?] husband. they merry another man. but I am not. so we must try hard to be nice to them Mrs Maude if we can. when you read this letter, and tell, your mother what I say to you. this is what our Mother and father say to us when we are going merring. to be king to how [who?] we merring him. we are the good best friends to its outher. your mother alwas send us some thing to the little. and some colders [clothes] for Wilfred. and dresses good for me. and I am sure you are going to be like your mother a king ladie. and I am going to ask you, if you have rain? this summer. we did not have anather rain out ther this summer. every things are dry with the hot sun. nother is green out here. . . . tell your mother we thunk her very much for the things what she send out for us. we sure like the candy. that time my brother was here and we got a box of things from your mother. and my brother so price [surprised]. and said o my. what a

24

nice good friends you have he said, they alwas send you some things. and he said some of the Hopi I naid has some friend to. but they dont get so many things from then. and here you get lot of thing from them. you has the nice good best friends you has. the colders [clothes] for Vivian and her father. some dresses good for you. said my brother. and he is looking at your mother picture. this what ny brother said to me tell your mother about it. and remember us all time. we remember you all the time, never forget you. ansure soon if you have time.

  your loving freind, Ethel Wilfred.

please tell your mother, to tell us, when they are coming out here. se we can now it.

Miss Ryan and Ethel Salyah and her two children—1927

Through letters like this, Ethel Salyah established a regular pattern of exchange incorporating the Melvilles as a kind of extended kin of the Salyah family; or, to put it another way, the Melvilles became willing agents for an emergent Hopi-Tewa trading network. Along with the commodities there was a reciprocal exchange of photographs as the Melville children grew and as new children were born to Ethel Salyah.

The fact that the Melvilles and the Salyahs continued their pattern of reciprocal gift exchange for so many years is particularly striking when one remembers that it was entirely fortuitous that they ever met and that, in actuality, the personal contact was so brief. Professor Melville, who served as navigator on the 1927 trip, had a semi-professional interest in geology and, of course, wanted to see the Grand Canyon and the other natural wonders of the west. He included the Hopi Mesas on his proposed route only because Dorothy Humes, of the First Mesa Baptist Mission, was an aunt of his daughter, Maud's, "chum Helen from Worcester." None of the Melvilles expected to stay at Hopi for more than a few days. And their extended stay at Hopi was in marked contrast to their brief stops at certain Pueblos in New Mexico. Maud Arnold recalls that, at San Ildefonso, they were made to understand that they were tourists: "Oh, that was horrible! All they wanted was money, money, money." They bought some pottery; but there was no social or cultural exchange, and the pottery was never valued by the Melvilles as much as their subsequent acquisitions at Hopi.

The Hopi area has always been isolated and remote; but in the first quarter of the twentieth century the power of Anglo-American society became increasingly evident in the Hopi area, a point that will be dealt with at some length in Chapter 4. Tourism, one manifestation of the Anglo presence, developed after the extension of rail service to the Southwest in the 1880s. But it was not until automobiles were available that tourists in significant numbers could stray away from the railroad lines to the remote villages of the Southwest. Therefore, although tourists streamed through the New Mexico pueblos, fewer penetrated to the Hopi Mesas. The Melvilles saw no other tourists during their stay at Polacca, according to Maud Arnold. They were not, however, the first Anglo visitors at Hopi, as is made clear in the following passage from a letter written by Mrs. Melville on June 24, 1927:

> Miss Ryan is so delighted to have us here, and says the Indians think we are real people, not just tourists. You see, we've been to all the Church meetings even tho we can't understand. She says it helps because so many painted tourists leave a wrong impression.

There may be some lingering doubts as to the degree to which the Melvilles were perceived as "real people" by the Hopis; but it is clear that they did their best to comply with and show respect for the wishes of the native inhabitants, just as they complied with the wishes of their missionary hosts in absenting themselves from all the "Indian" (non-Christian) ceremonies.

The respect which the Melvilles showed for the Hopis and Tewas and their cultural forms was not simply a manifestation of conventional good manners, however. The Melvilles had a kind of reverence for Southwestern Indian artists and their art with which they must have imbued the ceramics they were at such pains to acquire. For Mrs. Melville, at least, the ceramic pieces may have been tangible expressions of a heightened awareness which she evidently felt herself capable of achieving through Indian art. In this respect her response to Indian art was not unlike that of the Anglo "yearners" of the Taos and Santa Fe art colonies, who have identified with the eastern Pueblos since the World War I period (Simmons 1979:219–220).

Mrs. Melville's lectures on "Hopi Indians—the Modern Cliff Dwellers" and "Music of the Southwest Indians" were studded with such phrases as the Indian "art instinct." A passage from Curtis (1907) which appears in her lecture notes reads as follows:

> The wind sweeping the crags and whirling down the trail has carved its strange melody on the Indian's mind even as it has carved on the rocks in the curious erosion the record of its presence. Its echo is heard in the song of the Hopi through desert solitudes. There in that wide land under the

blaze of the Arizona sun, amid the shifting color of the tinted sands and the purple blue of the shadows must the songs be heard to be heard *truly*.

Such passages from Mrs. Melville's lectures suggest, not only that she endowed the Southwestern Indians with a romantic aura but that she perceived them as timeless, immutable inhabitants of a world that had changed little, if at all, since 1492. Another passage from her lecture notes is more explicit on this point:

There is a subtle charm about the Hopi and their high perched homes that is particularly delightful. No other place in our land affords such an opportunity to observe native Americans living as they lived before Columbus came.

For Mrs. Melville, the collection was not simply an array of beautiful objects to be viewed and appreciated. It was used as a set of visual aids to recapture for herself and her audiences what she felt could never be explicated with words alone. One of Mrs. Melville's favorite passages appears in her lecture notes as follows:

To put on paper the spirit of Hopi music is as impossible as to put on canvas the shimmer and glare of the desert (Curtis 1907).

The Collection in Worcester—1942

CHAPTER 3

ART, BUSINESS AND THE AMERICAN ROAD

TOURISTS AND TRADERS

The last half of the nineteenth century brought Anglo-American manufactured goods to the Southwest, first as a result of military occupation and later through civilian traders. The increasing dependence of the Pueblo peoples on such imported items as flour, sugar, coffee, yard goods, tools, and utensils caused a corresponding reduction in native reliance on their traditional technology. Rail service, which reached Flagstaff, Arizona in 1882, provided a firm link between the pueblos and the global economy.

The items of native manufacture which were collected by the late nineteenth century ethnographers and traders were functional crafts made for local consumption. Col. James Stevenson, for example, collected samples of traditional craft items in wood, stone, bone, textiles and ceramics at Zuni, Acoma, and Hopi as early as 1879 (Stevenson 1883); and Thomas V. Keam, who received a license to trade in the canyon east of the Hopi Mesas in 1875 (McNitt 1962:161), collected traditional Hopi pottery and other artifacts throughout the last quarter of the nineteenth century. Keam attemped to ease the economic transition of the Hopis, as a service to his Hopi clients and in his own enlightened self-interest, by encouraging Hopi craftsmen to produce standardized, mass-produced ceramic bowls, jars, and tiles for sale to tourists (Wade and McChesney 1980:9). These items were sold through traders, however, rather than directly to the tourists.

Motorized tourists appeared in the New Mexico pueblos in the 1920s, particularly perhaps, after the establishment of the Santa Fe Indian Art Market in 1922 (Wade 1976:83). Few of them penetrated to the remote Hopi Mesas in this period, however; and Maud Arnold Melville reports that her family saw no tourists there in 1927. Thus the tourist trade, in 1927, was burgeoning in the New Mexico pueblos, but was still in a developmental stage on the Hopi Reservation in Arizona.

Pueblo participation in the tourist business of the late nineteenth and early twentieth centuries consisted largely, at first, of the manufacture and sale of traditional craft items, but shifted more and more to the manufacture and sale of souvenirs and "Indian made" curios. The new tourists were less concerned with authenticity than were the earlier ethnographic collectors who had preceded them. The late nineteenth century tourist, according to Wade (1976: 51), "demanded a westernized version of the traditional crafts . . . and was mainly concerned that the item look 'Indian.' " The traders, of course, continued to mediate between the Indian artists and Anglo art consumers, encouraging and assisting the craftsmen in their transition to greater and faster production of objects that would appease the tourists' prodigious hunger for souvenirs.

Hopi (or Hopi-Tewa) participation in the tourist trade must have taken a new turn in 1904 when the El Tovar Hotel opened on the south rim of the Grand Canyon and employed Hopi potters and weavers to demonstrate their crafts (Wade 1976:69). This provided them an opportunity to sell newly made objects to tourists who had witnessed their manufacture. In this way the artists were directly and regularly exposed both to the tourists' tastes and preferences and to a cash economy.

In the context of the tourist market, Southwest Indian art moved inexorably in the direction of mass production. Impersonal, nonfunctional curios began to displace the larger, more labor intensive, more intricate and traditional craft items of an earlier period. According to Bartlett (1977:13),

> By 1920, pottery art had deteriorated in quality in favor of quantity. Every potter was busy turning out as many little curios as possible—ashtrays in the form of cowboy hats was a horrible example. . . . the quality of black paint had also declined, for it easily rubbed off.

See Plate 12 for one of these "horrible examples" which was collected by the Melvilles.

By the 1920s a number of collectors and *aficionados*, including Mary Colton, a founder of the Museum of Northern Arizona, were distressed at the deterioration of Indian art in the Southwest. Mrs. Colton attributed the decline to

> the introduction of commercial materials and to market pressure for curios rather than fine arts. She felt that Hopi art could be preserved by promoting traditional techniques and by encouraging a more sophisticated market (Breunig 1978:9).

What in fact Mrs. Colton and the staff of the Museum of Northern Arizona were proposing was that Hopi pottery be classified as an "art pottery" rather than a commercial ceramic. The concept of pottery as an art form was relatively recent, having developed during the British Arts and Crafts Movement of the 1870s and 1880s. The Rookwood Pottery, which was to become the foremost producer of art pottery in the United States, was founded in 1880 by a group of wealthy Cincinnati women. It was not, however, until the 1890s that pottery was firmly established as an art form in the United States. Rookwood pottery was exhibited in the Palace of Fine Arts at the Columbian Exposition in Chicago in 1893 (Peck 1968:47) and two years later Nampeyo demonstrated pottery at the Santa Fe Railroad Fair, also held in Chicago (Nequatewa 1943:42). Thus, a precedent had already been established for Hopi-Tewa pottery as an art form. The Indian-art pottery relationship was further reinforced by the Rookwood Indian portrait series produced in 1898.

After 1900 demand and distribution of art pottery increased, further promoted by the mail order catalogue. The 1904 Rookwood catalogue included a variety of elongated vases, including the tulip vase (Peck 1968:75–89). This may well have been the source of this form at Hopi. By the 1920s art pottery for home and garden was part of American *decor*; and Rookwood pottery was given formally to Heads of States (Peck 1968:106). It is not surprising, therefore, given the prestige of individually crafted pottery, that in 1919 the School of American Research, and later the Museum of Northern Arizona, would desire to promote Hopi-Tewa pottery as an art form. Traders had likewise seen the advantage of so classifying Indian pottery; hence their desire to have the pottery signed. Pottery signed by the individual craftsman became widespread only after the concept of pottery as an art form was established. As stated in the Rookwood Mail Order Catalogue:

A vase made at Rookwood under the conditions existing there is as much an object of art as a painted canvas or sculpture in marble or bronze. And the artist's signature upon the vase is as genuine a guarantee of originality (Peck 1968:74).

Spurred on by Mrs. Colton, the Museum of Northern Arizona took steps to establish Hopi-Tewa pottery as an art form in contrast to "commercial . . . curios." Toward this goal they instituted a "Hopi Craftsmen Exhibition" and a parallel Navajo exhibition designed to provide incentives for native artists to create what the museum staff regarded as high quality, traditional, handmade items, including of course items made of pottery. The Hopi exhibition or "Show" became an annual event beginning in 1930. Artists were encouraged to submit their best work; and there were cash awards and ribbons for first and second place winners in a variety of categories. Awards were intended to enhance the value and marketability of "good" pieces and reverse some of the less fortunate trends that curio production had initiated.

Information on the awards and categories of art in the first annual Hopi Craftsmen Exhibition of 1930 is not available; but for the second exhibition, in 1931, the "Divisions and Categories" were as indicated in Figure 1, below. The prizes listed in Figure 1 are approximate.

Divisions and categories	First Prize	Second Prize
Ceramics		
jars	$2.50–$3.00	$2.00
bowls	2.00	1.50
small pots/cups	1.50	1.00
tiles	1.00	.75
dippers	?	.50
Baskets	1.50–3.00	1.00–2.50
Blankets/Dresses	6.00–7.00	3.50–4.00
Belts	2.00–5.00	2.00
Other (dolls, drums, moccasins, paintings, etc.)	2.00–5.00	2.00–2.50

Figure 1. *Divisions, Categories and Prizes in the Hopi Craftsmen Exhibition of 1931*

Some measure of the inflation of Southwest Indian art prizes over the past 50 years may be obtained by comparing the 1931 awards with those of the 1982 Hopi Craftsmen Exhibition some fifty years later. The 1982 awards consisted of a $500 "division award" for best piece within a given division, $50 for first prize in any one category, and a $50 "division award" for the best item in the miscellaneous division. The categories in the miscellaneous division in 1982 were "quilts, embroidered shirts," and "pillows," none of which are traditional items. The first prize for each of these categories was $15. Most of the miscellaneous categories listed for the 1931 exhibition had achieved division status by 1982 (Anonymous 1982).

POLICIES AND PROCEDURES

The categories used to classify items entered in the 1978 Hopi Craftsmen Exhibition are more revealing, perhaps, than the awards presented in Figure 1. There are also policies and procedures that govern the eligibility of pieces and of artists to enter their work and policies relating to the selection of judges which have had an important bearing on Hopi art and the Southwestern Indian art business as they have developed over the past half a century.

Overall policy for the annual exhibits is set each year by the Museum of Northern Arizona, the sponsoring institution. This overall policy determines the rules for eligibility of artists and items, the categories to be judged, number of awards to be given, and method by which judges are to be selected. The official policy governing the 1978 Hopi Exhibition is given below as representative of recent policies.

Part 1 of "Policies and Procedures, 1978" is as follows:

> The function of the Hopi and Navajo shows is to foster greater public appreciation of the aesthetic, cultural and technical aspects of Hopi and Navajo arts and crafts. This includes encouraging the maintenance of high quality traditional arts and crafts, as well as encouraging innovative forms.

> The Museum endeavors to fulfill these functions in the most professional manner possible in keeping with current standards and Museum practices in the curatorial, exhibition design and educational realms (Anonymous 1978).

It may be worth noting here that this first paragraph calls for the encouragement of "traditional arts and crafts as well as . . . innovative forms," but gives no priority rating of either one over the other, so that judges are given no criteria for choosing between excellent "traditional" and excellent "innovative" entries.

Part 3 of "Policies and Procedures, 1978" relates to "Eligibility." To be eligible for the Hopi exhibition "one must ethnically be a Hopi. . . . Questions of eligibility are to be referred to [the tribal office]" (Anonymous 1978).

This statement makes no distinction between Hopis and Tewas or between the residents of the various pueblos and villages in which Hopis and Tewas reside. In providing only that the artists must be "Hopi" and that questions of eligibility are to be referred to the Tribal Office, it in fact assures that Tewas are eligible, since the Hopi Tribe has, since its inception, been dominated by the Hopis and Tewas of First Mesa, as will be made clear in Chapter 4.

Part 4 of "Policies and Procedures, 1978" addresses the question of eligibility of entries, and reads as follows:

> For the Hopi Show, entries will be accepted only from the maker or a member of his or her immediate family with permission of the maker. No entries will be accepted from dealers or agents, except tribal cooperatives or enterprises who can verify that the objects were made by tribal members. Hopi Show entries will be accepted on reservation collecting trips or at the Museum of Northern Arizona if delivered by or for the maker.

Both Part 3 and Part 4 make reference to the Hopi "tribe." Thus the policies regulating eligibility of both the art and the artists assume that the "Hopi Tribe" is a legitimate and viable organization. In fact, however, the "Hopi tribe" was created by the Federal Government to represent a constituency. Many of the groups within this constituency have consistently supported their local priesthoods but have declined to acknowledge any claim of legitimacy for the federally imposed tribal organization. This is a matter which will be addressed at some length in Chapter 4. For present purposes we need know only that the legitimacy of the tribe is currently very much at issue on the Hopi Reservation and that validation of objects and artists by "tribal" officials or "tribal" cooperatives does not guarantee their legitimacy as perceived by many Hopis.

Part 5 relates to the number of items which may be submitted to the exhibit by any one individual:

> As a general rule . . . the Museum will not set a limit on the number of entries from individuals. However, no more than three items per person per category will be accepted for judging (Anonymous 1978).

The fact that limits are imposed on the number of entries that may be made by or for any given artist requires, of course, that the artists be identified before their entries can be accepted. This raises the question as to whether a traditional artist who refused to sign her pieces and insisted on her anonymity could enter her work in the exhibit. One wonders also whether artists who collaborate, each performing a separate task, like Maria and Julian Martinez, feel constrained to identify their work with one of their number rather than admitting to a pattern of communally generated art which may be more pervasive in the pueblos than among Anglo artists.

Part 9 assigns responsibility for the selection of judges:

> Judges will be selected by the Curator of the Museum. They will be individuals with expertise in the categories to be judged.

Curiously enough, it was not until 1978, apparently, that any Indians served as judges in the Hopi Exhibition, either because the previous curators were unable to identify any Indians with sufficient expertise or because such people declined to serve.

Part 9 provides that only one first prize and one second prize is to be awarded in each category. These are to consist of a blue ribbon and a red ribbon, respectively. Honorable mentions (green ribbons) may be given to as many items as the judges see fit. A "special award" may be given to the most outstanding piece in any division.

In 1978 I was employed by the Museum of Northern Arizona to help produce the Hopi and Navajo Shows. The divisions and categories used for the Hopi "Show" were as follows:

Pottery
  Plain Redware
  Black on Red
  Polychrome
  White Slip
  Miniatures

Basketry
  Yucca Sifters
  Coil Placques
  Utilitarian Baskets
  Wicker Baskets

Jewelry
  Bracelets set with stone
  Bracelets—plain silver
  Belts
  Necklaces
  Flat ware
  Hollow ware
  Gold
  Miscellaneous

Textiles
  Non-traditional Women's Shawls
  Non-traditional White Kilts
  Wedding Sashes
  Hopi Belts
  Men's Embroidered Sashes
  Men's Embroidered Kilts
  Blankets
  Anklets
  Stockings

Kachinas

Paintings

Miscellaneous Items
  Rattles
  Bows and arrows
  Lightning Sticks
  Moccasins
  Gourds
  Bull-roarers
  Dance wands

Additional subcategories were used, as needed, to differentiate between sizes within a given category, e.g., small, medium, and large.

JUDGING

In 1978 the Curator of the Museum of Northern Arizona chose two Indian Americans to serve as judges together with four Anglos. Prior to that time, only Anglo Americans seem to have served as judges. These were, typically, well known dealers, gallery owners, and museum personnel. In 1978, the six judges included a Navajo weaver, who had demonstrated her art on the south rim of the Grand Canyon, and one other Indian, the Indian Arts Coordinator for the state of New Mexico. There were also four Anglo judges: a professor of Hopi language and linguistics from the University of Arizona, the professor's wife, a trading post owner, and the owner of a Scottsdale shop specializing in Southwestern Indian art. There was also a judge mediator to help resolve difficult problems.

Before proceeding to a general discussion of the criteria used in practice by the judges in the 1978 Hopi and Navajo Exhibitions it may be appropriate to outline a few cases which illustrate something of the range of considerations which entered into their deliberations.

In one case a Navajo judge, when presented with the Navajo weaving entries, gave a blue ribbon to a rug with a relatively simple "storm pattern" design and with corners that turned up because they were woven too tightly at the ends. She indicated that she gave this rug first prize because it was traditional and simple, "the way they used to make them." One of the Anglo judges was dismayed by this decision and remarked, out of earshot, that "It will never sell with those curly ends. It's a waste of a blue ribbon." Clearly, the Navajo judge gave precedence to "tradition" and "design"; the Anglo judge favored craftsmanship and marketability. Recall that the "Policies and Procedures, 1978" came out strongly in favor of "tradition" and "innovation" and the "aesthetic, cultural and technical aspects of Hopi and Navajo arts and crafts." But since no priorities were given, it is not surprising that different judges gave different weightings to these criteria. The criterion of marketability invoked by the Anglo judge ("It will never sell. . . .") is nowhere mentioned in the "Policies and Procedures"; but it is easy to understand how it might influence a judge who had built up a business based on his knowledge of the Indian art market.

While it is quite understandable that a Navajo judge in 1978 should consider the storm pattern "traditional," her grandparents in the 1920s would scarcely have agreed. The storm pattern is a western Navajo design which developed in the early twentieth century in the area around Tuba City. According to Dedera (1975:65–66),

> No style has attracted more contradictory lore. One tale ascribes the origin to a pattern printed on sacks of flour shipped to western Navajoland in the early days. Then again, since J. B. Moore of Crystal, New Mexico, included a storm pattern in his 1911 catalog, it may have sprung from one of his patterns. Still another possibility was a Tonalea trader with a keen appreciation for what paleface rug buyers expected in the way of Indian symbolism.

All three of these suggested origins attribute the design in part to Anglo influence. Indeed, the very fact that the storm pattern has a border is proof of the influence of Anglo traders. According to Charles Avery Amsden, the classic authority on Navajo weaving,

> Blankets with borders (rugs, most of them are) unquestionably do mark a style, entirely consistent in both time and character . . . from 1900 to 1920 few rugs left the loom without at least one neat strip of color along each

34

edge as a border. . . . the bordered style. . . . has all the nondescript character of the American culture which fostered it, for this style is beyond much question a white man's imposition on the nascent rug business, since all our pictures are framed and our rugs bordered (Amsden 1934:215–216, as quoted in Wade 1976:66).

Thus the storm pattern rug that won first prize in 1978 because it was "the way they used to make them" conformed to a tradition that did not crystalize before the twentieth century and clearly bears the stamp of Anglo influence.

In 1979 two Navajo judges selected an extremely well woven pictorial rug for first place. They especially appreciated the content of the pictorial. The museum personnel and collectors were distressed, however, because the colors were too bright and because "cute" bunny rabbits, flowers and butterflies had supplanted the more conventional subject matter of pictorials—*hogans*, pickups, and corn motifs. In this case, the Navajo judges opted for craftsmanship and creativity, while the "experts" united behind the banner of muted colors and what have come to qualify as "traditional" Navajo graphics.

Judging yucca sifters at the Hopi Show—1978

On another occasion the judges were pondering an array of some 50 Hopi yucca sifters. They felt that all the entries were of uniform quality with one exception, which stood out very sharply from the others. This particular sifter had the virtue of being perfectly round, which accounted for the fact that it was woven so evenly. I had noticed this piece the day before and picked it up, to find that it was unusually heavy. During the judging, this perfectly round, heavy sifter caught the eye of one of the Indian judges, who remarked that it had a very nice "feel." She went on to say that she could "see using this as a sifter because it has this weight about it that would lend itself very nicely to sifting." Then she discovered the reason for the extra weight and perfect symmetry. A copper or brass ring had been used to form the rim instead of the traditional bent stick. The judge said that, if she were to make a yucca sifter, that was exactly how she would do it. She was delighted with this innovation, despite the fact that the piece was not made entirely from native materials. She gave it, however, only an honorable mention. Her rationale was that metal rings were not legitimate components of yucca sifters and that, since symmetry was more difficult to achieve with sticks than with metal rings, this sifter could not be considered a fair test of its maker's craftsmanship.

Although the Hopi Exhibit is explicitly intended to encourage "innovative forms," and although the very nature of a competitive show, judged by "experts" appointed by the curator of a museum, could not fail to impose new standards of excellence in Indian art, the basic objective of the exhibits is, and always has been, to somehow support traditional art forms. As we have seen in the case of the storm pattern rug with curled up corners, the judges tend to support tradition. Tradition, for museum personnel and art dealers, however, tends to reside in specific colors, forms, substances, and techniques, e.g., corn plant designs, vegetable dies, and sticks for the frame of sifters. Native artists, on the other hand, tend to think of tradition as (to use the Navajo judge's words) "the way they used to make them." Thus the Hopi show is guaranteed to uphold tradition; but one is never certain which traditions will be upheld, the Indians' or the collectors'.

"Innovative forms," which the first paragraph of the "Policies and Procedures, 1978" commends so highly, are sometimes approved by the judges. At the 1978 Hopi Exhibition the judges showed great interest in certain shapes of pottery that they had not seen for a long time or had never seen at all. They seemed much more tolerant, if not enthusiastic, about new shapes than about new designs, which they tended to reject summarily. Whatever its shape, however, the judges insisted on overall symmetry and rejected any pot that was bottom heavy or visibly assymmetrical, or anything that would rock back and forth on its base. They favored pots with smooth, slick surfaces without fire clouds or other "flaws" and with designs painted evenly with fine, clear-cut lines. Occasionally a judge would test a pot by striking a forefinger against its side. The resulting sound would indicate whether the pot was cracked. A good, clear ring is evidence that the pot is uncracked, was fired at a high temperature and is consequently durable. The finger test is also used as a measure of the thickness of a vessel's walls. Thin walls are considered superior to thick ones.

The judges often remarked about how difficult it must have been to make a given piece and how long the artist must have taken to make it. Prizes were often awarded on the basis of their presumed difficulty and estimated production time. A set of instructions on how to judge Hopi pottery which appeared in *Plateau Magazine*, the Museum of Northern Arizona's quarterly, includes the following dictum:

Consider the complexity of the design, remembering that the more difficult and time-consuming the design, the more valuable is the item (Hitchcock 1977:25).

As we have seen in the case of the Navajo pictorial rug, however, difficulty, craftsmanship, and time expended count for very little if the design elements violate what the judges perceive as "tradition."

The pottery that has been submitted for competition in the Hopi Craftsmen Exhibition over the past few years is quite different from the Sikyatki Revival vessels that were collected by the Melvilles in the 1920s and '30s. The modern pots are very smooth and appear "slick." Contemporary artists and collectors profess an admiration for prehistoric Sikyatki Polychrome and for early Sikyatki Revival wares; but, if such pots were made today and submitted for competition, very few would be considered for first place. A half century of juried competitions presided over by museum-appointed experts has, understandably, developed its own traditions and its own standards of excellence, both explicit and implicit. There is no doubt that Hopi pottery has changed. Nor is there any doubt that the artists, judges, and collectors have all kept, more or less, in step with new developments so that there continues to be a rough consensus. This was, after all, one of the central, though implicit, purposes of the exhibits. The exhibitions educate dealers, collectors, and tourists, as well as the artists, creating a kind of resonance between these disparate groups.

Sikyatki Revival wares at the Hopi Show—1978

One additional criterion is often used in judging Hopi pottery, although it does not appear in the "Policies and Procedures, 1978" and I know of no instance in which it has been invoked by judges. We may assume that the Hopi-Tewa artists are well aware of it, however. This is the criterion of scarcity. The Hopi-Tewas of First Mesa control the supply of "Hopi" pottery. It would seem that they contrive to produce a supply that invariably falls short of the demand, thus ensuring a tidy income for themselves, regardless of what happens at the Hopi Craftsmen Exhibition.

Having personally attended and assisted in the production of the Hopi and Navajo Exhibitions for several years, and having observed the judges at their work, I have found that I can predict with considerable accuracy which of a set of entries will win awards and which will not. My experience suggests also that the cumulative decisions made by judges over the years have had considerable influence on the current standards of excellence for Hopi art, which are, consciously or unconsciously, endorsed by the artists as well as dealers, critics, and museum personnel. It is abundantly clear to me that these decisions by judges, though not always governed directly by self-interest, are usually compatible with the interests of influential figures in the Indian art business, since it is precisely this Indian art business which has been best represented, historically, among those chosen to judge.

Finally, it is not at all clear to me that Anglo commercialism has corrupted, manipulated or exploited the "naive" Indian artists. Hopi-Tewa artists can be as shrewd as any Anglo dealer; and the Indian art business serves their interests as well as those of the dealers, perhaps because these canny, Hopi-Tewa traders, like *really* good traders the world over, have been so successful in identifying themselves to Anglos as guileless romantics. Who would ever believe that these "Hopi artists" could create and maintain a First Mesa monopoly of a prestigious product line for which Anglo consumers, on the advice of their own experts, pay thousands of dollars, most of which may never be reported to the Internal Revenue Service.

CHAPTER 4

THE AMERICAN ROAD TO FREEDOM AND ENLIGHTENMENT

In this account of Hopi relationships with Anglo society, I will make no mention of the early Spanish contacts or the sporadic, nineteenth century visits of such Anglo American travelers as General Nelson A. Miles, Colonel James Stevenson, and Frank Hamilton Cushing. I will focus instead on the concerted, programatic attempts by missionaries and agents of the United States government to destroy or modify native Hopi political, social, religious, and economic institutions as a step toward their political integration, if not their complete assimilation, into the American mainstream. These attempts were implemented by a varied assortment of missionaries, Indian agents, soldiers and visionaries, beginning in the late nineteenth century and continuing well into the twentieth. They have had enormous impact on the Hopi villages, for although no one of these programs can be said to have been an unqualified success, it is certain that Anglo interference, beginning in the 1880s, created cleavages in Hopi society which are very evident today.

From the opening of the Keams Canyon Boarding School in 1887 to the creation of the Hopi Tribal Council and Constitution in 1936, missionaries, school teachers, military personnel, and Indian agents cajoled and coerced Hopi "pagans" to adopt a "civilized," Christian way of life, and to move down from their mesas and onto the American road, which promised an advanced technology, the freedom of Western democratic institutions, and the enlightenment that comes with the adoption of Christianity and the English language. But these assimilationists did not have an easy time. Many Hopis clung to their own institutions and rejected the "opportunities" that were offered to them. In time, however, schools, the Bible, and majority rule were introduced, each with some degree of success, particularly on First Mesa. The Hopis of Sichomovi and Walpi, and the Tewas of Hano showed the greatest enthusiasm for these alien Anglo institutions; and a schism between them and the Hopis of Second and Third Mesa has developed and grown inexorably wider and deeper over the last century.

MISSIONARIES

Formal relationships between the Hopis and the United States date back to 1850, when a delegation of seven Hopi and Tewa leaders went to Santa Fe, two years after the Mexican-American War, to ask John S. Calhoun, the first federal Indian agent in the Southwest, for military protection from Navajo raids (Dockstader 1979:524). Sporadic visits to the Hopi villages by Anglo explorers took place over the following decade; but the first serious attempt by Anglo Americans to bring about lasting changes in Hopi society occurred in 1858, when Jacob Hamlin and other representatives of the Church of Jesus Christ of Latter Day Saints began to proselytize on the Hopi mesas. These missionaries were asked to leave not long afterward; and, although three Hopis later accompanied them to Salt Lake City, few changes seem to have been wrought by the Mormon Mission in this period. Indeed, ten years later, in 1872, J. H. Beadle "failed to discover the slightest trace of any religion" among the Hopis (Donaldson 1893:17). In 1875 the Mormons established a mission at Moenkopi, a Hopi farming village some distance from the mesas; but they never succeeded in converting any substantial number of Hopis. According to Dockstader (1979:526):

> The major effect of the Mormon mission was the degree of protection that it offered from the Navajos of the western region. Surprisingly enough, there was very little interaction between the two groups, and almost no successful conversions to Mormonism took place. In effect, the two peoples lived side by side with little reaction. The one primary result of this coexistence was the slow takeover of Hopi land by the Mormons, until the Hopis were reduced to a position of relative peonage on their own lands.
>
> In 1878 the Mormons established Tuba City as their major outpost in northern Arizona and began to expand toward the [Hopi] villages. . . .

Acting on instructions from the Foreign Mission Board of the General Mennonite Conference, H. R. Voth established a Mennonite Mission at Oraibi, on Third Mesa, in 1893 (Dockstader 1979:527). Unlike J. H. Beadle, he soon discovered the indigenous religion, for which he developed considerable respect. His inquiries, however, produced information that was often "misleading, distorted, and unreliable. . . . the Priests were not very anxious to furnish me anything that I wanted to use to undermine their religion" (James 1974: 153). Voth had studied medicine for two years and found that his medical skills gave him access to Hopi society. In his journal he mentions treating many families and, at one time, over 80 cases of measles. Thus, by mixing Christianity with outpatient therapy, he gradually succeeded in penetrating the "hostile" community of Oraibi.

In 1901 a Mennonite church was built at Oraibi by Voth and his converts. This contributed to the polarization of Oraibi which resulted in the emigration of the "hostile" faction in 1906 and a bitter dispute which has never been resolved. The destruction by lightning of the Mennonite church in 1942 was, no doubt, interpreted by many Hopis as a dramatic vindication of the orthodox Hopi religion (Dockstader 1979:528).

Upon her graduation from the Baptist Missionary Training School in 1898, Abigail Johnson was commissioned to work among the Cheyennes and Arapahos. In 1901, the same year in which Voth erected his Mennonite church at Oraibi, she was transferred to the Hopi Reservation (Means 1960:45). On her arrival she found that hymns and Bible readings were already in use in the classrooms of both Polacca, where a government day school had been built in 1894, and Keams Canyon, where a government school had been established at the old Keam Trading Post in 1887 (Dockstader 1979:527). A number of itinerant evangelists had visited First Mesa, and the Women's National Indian Association had established a short-lived mission at Second Mesa in 1887 (Wyckoff n.d. chapter 3:37); but, at the time of Miss Johnson's arrival, there was but one convert to Christianity on First Mesa (Means 1960:54).

At Polacca, the "progressive" village at the foot of First Mesa,

Miss Johnson thrilled with horror as she looked at the very tools of a false religion. Later missionaries, with a broader knowledge of comparative reli-

Members of the First Mesa Baptist Church, Polacca—1929. Church members mentioned in the text include 1. Hongavi (Judge Hooker), 2. Takala (Ruth's husband), 3. Myra, 4. Sellie, 5. Sehepmana (Hongavi's wife), 6. Edwin (Hattie Carl's husband), 7. Myrtle Ransier (Abigail Johnson's friend who worked at Polacca after Miss Johnson was transferred to Second Mesa), 8. Ruth, and 9. Ethel Ryan (Reverend Roger Ramsel, personal communication).

41

gion, might see in these tools a blind approach to the one God. Miss Johnson experienced only repugnance, together with a great thankfulness that she was privileged to bring light into such darkness (Means 1960:59).

Together with Miss Schofield, another Baptist missionary, Johnson ascended First Mesa to convert the heathen. She succeeded in persuading a few Hopis and Tewas to move down to Polacca. Others refused to move, but tolerated her visits. She was given a Hopi name, "Yellow Leaf," and assigned to the Mustard Clan. Despite the fact that she considered the Hopi kinship system to be "part of the dark religion" (Means 1960:64), she accepted adoption into the clan, hoping to win approval of herself and her religion.

Expediency also prompted her to learn the Hopi language, at a time when many missionaries perceived Indian languages more as an impediment to progress than a means of communication. Her effort to learn Hopi was appreciated, according to Means: "It was a subtle compliment on her part, and their delight at her effort encouraged her in the task" (Means 1960:62). Means interprets her adoption into the Mustard Clan and the Hopis' "delight" at her efforts to learn their language, as evidence of rapport between Johnson and the Hopis. "If her bright, inquiring eyes upon them sometimes made them flinch," she wrote (1960:63), "she had nevertheless already demonstrated that nothing was too hard or disagreeable for her to do for them."

In 1907, six Hopis were baptized on Second Mesa. According to the church records, the participants in the Baptism were "manhandled" by "hostile" Hopis (Means 1960:71). Another "Believer's Baptism" was soon held at Polacca, where a married couple, Sehepmana and Hongavi were baptized soon after. Hongavi, who was known to government agents at Keams Canyon as "Judge Hooker," was a man who understood the value of American style justice and assisted the government in maintaining "law and order."

Between 1910 and 1920 the Baptists disseminated the Gospel to a number of Hopis and Tewas at Polacca, below First Mesa, and at the Sunlight Mission, below Second Mesa. And Abigail Johnson and her associates climbed the trails with megaphones to bring their message to those who stayed on the mesas. Most church activities were curtailed in 1918 as a result of the influenza epidemic and the severe winter, both of which made it difficult to hold street meetings (Means 1960:91); but the church records for the year 1918 radiate optimism:

> The Christians have been doing more systematic personal work than ever before. Each one who is able to work . . . has a given number of non-Christians to whom he or she is to carry the Gospel every week if at all possible (Means 1960:87).

During this period, according to Means, Johnson overcame her initial revulsion and grew to accept the Hopis and Tewas "as her own people" and came "to love their desert home" (Means 1960:83).

In the 13 years that elapsed after the conversion of Sehepmana and Hongavi in 1907 only 32 Hopis and Tewas were baptized at Polacca and the Sunlight Mission. As the church grew, it established a laundry, with assistance from

The Melville camp between the Baptist Church and the laundry in Polacca—1927

the federal government, thus becoming a center for social activities as well as an outpost of Christendom.

> It was a normal and pleasant thing for them to listen to a Christian message and join in the singing while their washing dried in the brilliant Arizona sun" (Means 1960:87).

The federal superintendent, Leo Crane, appealed to the Baptists to provide medical assistance to the people of First and Second Mesas; and the resulting efforts by the missionaries brought them into an increasingly close alignment with the agency. This cooperative spirit continued when the government, itself, began to provide health care in 1929. According to Means,

> Before [Nurse Esther Sandstrom's] advent, the Hopis had recourse to two groups in sickness and death: the school people and the missionaries. The reliance on the mission had been important to its work, early winning the trust of the people. Miss Sandstrom realized and appreciated Miss Johnson's quick withdrawal from the nurse's field of action, and her friendly intermediacy in helping the people make full use of the nurse's knowledge and skill (1960:98).

Thus between the influenza epidemic of 1918 and the arrival of Nurse Sandstrom in 1929, the federal government and the Baptists developed a system of complementary programs, cooperating in their efforts to achieve their common goal—the introduction of Anglo American culture to the Hopis and Tewas.

The United Presbyterian Church established a mission at Ganado, 50 miles east of Keams, in 1921. Pliny Adams, who had converted to the Baptist Church in 1910 (Means 1960:104), sent his children to school at the Ganado Mission, where they were taught English and Christianity. He served as a part-time missionary for the Women's American Baptist Home Mission Society, holding evening prayer meetings and spreading the Word with the help

43

of a portable organ. Other members of the Adams family were also advocating Jesus and the American road on Second Mesa (Means 1960:107–110). Thus, by the time of the Melvilles' arrival in 1927, there were Christian missions or churches at Ganado, Polacca, the Sunlight Mission, Oraibi, and Bacabi. Oraibi had been torn apart; and native, as well as Anglo, Christians were disseminating the gospel with the aid of megaphones and portable organs to anyone who would listen. Small wonder, perhaps, that the Melvilles felt constrained to attend only Christian services; for virtually all of the Hopis and Tewas, by 1927, were committed to one or the other of two rival camps.

INDIAN AGENTS

Some measure of the effectiveness of Federal Indian policy in the nineteenth century can be inferred from the fact that the drought-stricken Hopis sent a delegation to request famine relief in 1866 from authorities in New Mexico who referred them to the Governor of Arizona Territory in Prescott. Surprised by their appearance and misunderstanding the purpose of the Hopi emissaries, the authorities in Prescott had them arrested and put in jail. Although they were released soon after, this episode did little to inspire confidence in Anglo administrators.

An independent Hopi agency was created in 1869. Between 1869 and 1889 there was a rapid turnover of agents, most of whom were absentees. This only served to prolong the uncertainty and vacillation that marked Hopi relationships with the federal government.

A reservation consisting of a rectangle measuring approximately 55 by 70 miles was created by executive order for "the Hopis and other Indians" in 1882; but this somewhat belated recognition of the Hopis' proprietary interest in the area failed to bring prestige to the agency. Lt. John G. Bourke, who visited the Hopi villages in 1881, described the agent, a Mr. Sullivan, as a

> kind-hearted, superannuated gentleman, about seventy years old, honest and well-meaning, but not able to do much physical or mental labour, and, as goes without saying, entirely without influence over the Indians, whom he was supposed to manage (Bourke 1884:83).

The Hopis, according to Bourke, cared "but little for the agency or anybody connected with it," and as a result, the government personnel "possess the slightest influence over their charge, and might as well be in Nova Zembla for all the good they effect." He spoke of the agency as using "slouchy ill-judged methods" as compared with the "business-like ideas predominating in the Mormon management" (Bourke 1884:79).

Bourke's account suggests that the Hopi villages differed considerably in their attitudes toward Anglos in 1881. On Second Mesa he noted American-made agricultural tools and at Oraibi, on Third Mesa, he attributed "great influence" to the Mormons (Bourke 1884:330). But while he detected some "progress" on Second and Third Mesas, he was most impressed with the First Mesa villages, which had made substantial strides toward "civilization" despite their ineffectual agent. At Walpi, on First Mesa, Bourke was "met with urbane treatment" and, much to his surprise "experienced no molestation whatever" (1884:105–107). Indeed, he would have been "delighted to remain all night had it not been for the stench and heat, which were simply overpowering." At Sichomovi, Bourke and his companion, Dr. Sullivan, were entertained by a man named Tochi, at whose house they dined. Bourke found the meal "meager in quantity and inferior in quality," but only, perhaps, because his host was overzealous in his attempts to serve a "civilized" supper:

It would not do to wound the feelings of Tochi, who had acted from a very hospitable impulse, and, as the affair had not a few ludicrous features, we were soon laughing hilariously at the grotesqueness of the situation. For, I should say, that Tochi was not making any endeavor to give us a Moqui [Hopi] collation; that would have been good enough; but in his ambitious straining after the white man's ways, the idea had seized upon him of giving an American supper, and here it was, in all its grandeur as he understood it, served up in tin cups gathered from all sources, or empty fruit cans received from the agent for past personal services (Bourke 1884:103).

Thus in 1881 there may already have been a perceptible difference in attitudes toward the American road between First Mesa, where Bourke was received with courtesy and even hospitality, however "ludicrous," and the other two mesas, where the presence of agricultural implements of American manufacture was the major mark of "progress."

In 1886, five years after Bourke's visit, Keam wrote the Commissioner of Indian Affairs suggesting that his trading post could be converted into a boarding school for 50 students. He said that at least that many could be enrolled "as the Moquis [Hopis] . . . living in the western half of the reservation are constantly making inquiries about the school here" (Keam 1886). James Gallagher, the newly appointed agent, supported this proposal in his annual report early in 1887 and forwarded a petition to Washington signed by 20 Hopis and Tewas including Sapula, a Walpi resident, and Honani of Shongopavi, on Second Mesa. In October of 1887, 52 children were enrolled, and a few years later it was confidently predicted that the graduates of the Keams school would carry

with them an education and habits of life far superior to any they had heretofore enjoyed, and no one can fail to believe, or to hope at least, that the 103 children now present in the school, returning to their homes imbued with another and better civilization, will produce much good (Donaldson 1893:37).

The school was, indeed, a success insofar as First Mesa, and particularly, perhaps, the Tewas were concerned. Keams Canyon was within 12 miles of the First Mesa villages, which soon met their quotas for school attendance. In 1890 a group of Hopis, and presumably Tewas, visited the Carlisle Indian School in Pennsylvania at government expense. The visitors were so impressed by the industrial arts program at Carlisle as to request that a similar program be instituted at Keams Canyon (James 1974:111). This request was never acted upon; but two additional government schools were established at Polacca and at Oraibi in 1894 (Dockstader 1979:527).

While the boarding schools were well attended by First Mesa children, they were vigorously resisted by Second Mesa and, with the exception of the "friendly" minority at Oraibi, by Third Mesa as well. Oraibi having failed to meet its quota of students for the Keams Canyon school, the U.S. Army dispatched a unit to that village. Col. H. C. Corbin, with four troops of cavalry and two Hotchkiss guns, entered Oraibi on July 2, 1891. Keam, who participated in the action, described the incident as follows:

> After saying a few words to them, I escorted them to the troops, where they were made prisoners and heard some good advice from Colonel Corbin. They were quite sullen and refused to answer questions. The order was now given to mount, and we rode up into the village, taking the whole command, with the 2 Hotchkiss guns. Here we took the war chief and his son prisoners. Both were finer and better looking men than any of the others. The son, on being asked what he had to say, replied: "I was prepared to fight the few soldiers that were here some days ago, because I thought we could kill them and drive them away; now, however, it would be useless. I never saw so many Americans before. You have my friends prisoners and I am not able to fight all these soldiers; take me, as I am in your power." The troops were then arranged in front of the village, and after Colonel Corbin had explained to the people what was to be done with the prisoners, and impressed them with obedience to their chief, La-lo-la-my, he said he would show them what would have been done with the Hotchkiss guns if they had offered resistance. I had started toward the guns to witness the firing, when I heard loud shouting, yelling, and screaming from the Indians, and as I turned saw an Indian pursued by a soldier jump off the mesa. It was one of the prisoners escaped, and the excitement was great for a while. He succeeded in getting away, and has not yet been caught. A strict guard was kept on the others, who were brought safely to camp and well guarded that night (Donaldson 1893:38).

The "La-lo-la-my" of Keams' account was, no doubt, a man known as Lololoma, the head chief of Oraibi, the largest of the Hopi villages. Lololoma had gone to Washington in 1884 with Keam and a delegation of Hopis (McNitt 1962:192). Although prior to this trip he had advocated resistance to Anglo pressures, the trip to Washington convinced him that the Hopis should send their children to school (Titiev 1944:72). Thus no less a figure than the head chief of Oraibi was advocating the American road at the time of Corbin's raid. Hopi resistance did not crumble, however; the conservative majority (Titiev 1944:82), led by Lomahongyoma, a native priest of Oraibi, kept their children out of school, and the quotas were not met. In 1892 the superintendent reported that another show of force was required "to compel them" to send their children to school (James 1974:112); but the "hostiles" remained adamant, opposing not only compulsory education but the implementation of the Dawes Act of 1887 which, if implemented, would have resulted in the division of clan-owned land and its allotment to individual Hopis. The intransigence of Lomahongyoma and his "hostiles" succeeded, ultimately, in preventing the individual allotment of Hopi lands.

Donaldson's census report of 1893 gives a total population for "the 7 Moqui Pueblos in 1890" of 1,996. Of these, 51 could speak English—23 from First

Mesa, 28 from Oraibi, none from other villages; 33 could read English—21 from First Mesa, 12 from Oraibi, none from other villages; 25 could write English—22 from First Mesa, 3 from Oraibi; none from other villages; and 93 were "at school"—38 from First Mesa, 44 from Oraibi, and 11 from other villages. Donaldson's statistics clearly reflect the pro-school sentiments of First Mesa and of Lololoma's "friendlies" at Oraibi, and the anti-school sentiments of all other Hopis. Figure 2, below, shows relevant statistics, drawn from Donaldson's report for the Tewas, the First Mesa Hopis, Oraibi, all other villages, and for all "Moquis" (Hopis and Tewas combined).

	FIRST MESA		SECOND & THIRD MESA		TOTAL "MOQUIS"
					(Hopis & Tewas)
	Tewas	Hopis	Oraibi	Other Villages	
AT SCHOOL	18	20	44	11	93
WRITE ENGLISH	12	10	3	0	25
READ ENGLISH	12	9	12	0	33
SPEAK ENGLISH	13	10	28	0	51
TOTAL POPULATION	161	335	905	595	1996

Figure 2. *Population, school attendance, and English language proficiency data for selected residential groups on the Hopi Reservation, drawn from Donaldson (1893:45)*

As a result of their opposition to allotment and their active interference with the surveying of Hopi land preparatory to allotment, a number of the Oraibi "hostiles" were imprisoned at Fort Wingate. Continued resistance to the allotment program, and no doubt the school attendance issue, led to the arrest of Lomahongyoma and 18 of his associates, who were transported to Alcatraz Island where they were imprisoned for seven months. They were released on August 7, 1895, "for good behavior" (James 1974:114; Dockstader 1979:527).

The polarization of Oraibi reached its climax a decade later. Titiev's summary of the split is as follows:

From 1900 to 1905 tension between the Hostile and Friendly factions had seriously disrupted village life: even religious ceremonies were not free from interference. To gather strength and support, Lomahongyoma invited a number of sympathetic Hopi people from Shongopavi [on Second Mesa] to settle at Oraibi. Outraged at the distribution of their lands to Second Mesa villagers, the Friendlies sought to evict the newcomers. On September 8, 1906, in a memorable clash, they engaged the Hostile forces in a violent push-of-war and forced them back. As agreed, the 298 Hostile members packed their belongings and left Oraibi forever. They went to a site about seven miles northwest on Third Mesa, where they established a new village, Hotevilla. . . . The Friendlies, numbering about 324, stayed behind with Tawaquaptewa . . . as village chief. . . .

The next year, during the arguments over Bureau of Indian Affairs land-allotment efforts, some dissidents tried to return to Oraibi, but their request was refused and they eventually settled nearby, where they built the present-day village of Bacabi (Dockstader 1979:529, citing Titiev 1944).

The unreconstructed "hostiles" of Hotevilla continued to subvert the government's education program and, in 1911, the army was once more called upon to enforce the truancy regulation (Dockstader 1979:530). The Hopi agent in this period, Leo Crane, was hardly a man to mollify the dissidents. In 1912 he reported that the Hopis "live on a moral plane little above their livestock" (James 1974:165).

A decade later Crane's successor to the post of Hopi agent, Superintendent Daniel, showed the same insensitivity when he ordered the delousing of the Hopis. On June 10, 1921 a large vat was filled with sheep-dip and the Hopi men, women, and children were forced into and through it. Violet Pooley-ama, an unwilling participant in this proceeding, described the episode as follows:

> . . . Agent Daniel from Keams Canyon came to Hotevilla with all the white men he could get and some Indians under his hire. He told us there was sickness everywhere in Arizona and that he had orders to spray our houses and to see that we all took a bath in disinfectant. These white men sprayed our houses, often spoiling great amounts of our corn and dried meat. Then they made a big bath like the one they dip the sheep in. They filled this with sheep-dip. They started putting our men and boys in it as if they were sheep. They took the women and girls and put them in it, too. When the women fought with them they often threw them into the sheep-dip clothes and all. Sometimes they tore the clothes off the women and girls. It was not good for those men to look upon the bodies of our women and girls. They took old grandmothers and little girls they took everybody and threw them in the dirty sheep-dip. All the time the white men were laughing and making fun of them.

> Our old chief, Youkeoma, and the few men who were in the village when this happened tried to stop the white men, but they were unable to stop them. The white men were armed with heavy sticks like baseball bats and they would hit our men over the head with them. One man, Tuvenqumb-tewa, was hit over the head so hard that his head was split open and he was dead for nearly two hours. When he came alive again they put handcuffs on him and on another man and hung them to a horn of a saddle and sent them to the jail in Keams Canyon. Because they fought against the white men doing things to us, ten of our men of our village were put in jail in Keams Canyon. They are still there. Besides the two men they hung from the saddle of the horse, they took to the jail our chief, Youkeoma, and Henry Dalamanewa, Ralph Lomawyma, William Bahesie, Cochmasa, and Sacgyesva.

> Do you wonder now that the people of Hotevilla tremble when they see white people coming to our village? Why don't they leave us to ourselves? We were so happy before the white man came, but if we must go to school, why don't they build us a school with all the grades somewhere near our villages so that we can see our children every day? If Washington must send a man to look after us, why cannot we have a good man, a kind man who understands the Hopi people? (James 1974:180)

THE INDIAN REORGANIZATION ACT

When John Collier took office as the new Commissioner of Indian Affairs in 1933 he promptly denounced the Indian policy of the previous administration. His testimony before Congress on the question of reform faulted the federal government for suppressing native religions, for prohibiting Indians from speaking their own languages, and for attempting to force them to comply with Anglo American beliefs and practices and abandon their own. Cultural diversity was regarded by Collier as vitally important to the American experience; and the promotion of Indian American culture had top priority in the first year of his administration. Indian Americans were to experience "cultural liberation," free, for the first time in over a hundred years, from the absolutism of Indian agents and an ethnocentric Indian policy. The legislative vehicle for the new "cultural self-determination" was the Indian Reorganization Act, or Wheeler-Howard Act, of 1934.

The Indian Reorganization Act was designed to assure some degree of self-government to Indian American groups and to promote greater participation by such groups in shaping their future relationships with American society. "Tribal" groups were identified and encouraged to write constitutions, elect Councils empowered to govern by majority rule, and form corporations to manage reservation resources.

It is significant that, under the act, the Secretary of the Interior retained certain powers, including the power to veto tribal constitutions and the right to determine how often a tribal council would meet, how powerful its chairman should be, and whether or not a council could approve leases. The act also provided that a tribal council could not retain legal counsel without prior consultation with Washington. Collier defended these provisions as wise precautions, given the fact that the new tribal councils were inexperienced, fledgling governments. Since 1934, however, many have argued that these limitations on the powers of tribal councils were only a more sophisticated expression of the same old, high-handed paternalism that had characterized federal Indian policy in previous decades.

Critics of the act found that self-government was not only compromised by bureaucratic limitations, but was limited as well by the way in which it was defined in the act. Each community was to be governed by a centralized council, a new and unprecedented body for many Indian American groups, and was to make its decisions by majority vote, a method which was entirely alien to many Indian American communities in which consensus leadership was a highly developed art. Moreover, the management of tribal land and other tribal resources by the tribe was contingent on the creation of a corporate structure with a legally valid charter. Thus the Indian Reorganization Act required a tribal council, a written constitution, and a corporate structure as essential for Indians to exist as corporate groups in American society regardless of the fact that these institutional structures were imposed by an Anglo government on societies to which they were alien, if not outright antithetical.

The Indians were understandably uneasy about the Indian Reorganization

Act; but Collier reassured them. No legislation, he said, would be forced upon groups that did not want to adopt the new reforms. He also made assurances that the Bureau of Indian Affairs would be sensitive to the many differences between Indian American societies. For the first time, he said, a federal Indian policy was to be administered with the best interests of the Indians in mind.

As we have seen, the Hopis and Tewas had a long history of dispute and open conflict over the issue of how they should respond to the Anglo presence and Anglo innovations on the reservation. While some, particularly those on First Mesa and at Polacca, had accepted various programs introduced by missionaries and federal educational and medical programs, others clung to what they regarded as their aboriginal heritage and studiously rejected any and all aspects of what they perceived as an alien way of life. In addition to the perceptible, statistical differences between the three mesas which appear in Table 1, at least for the 1890s, there were profound political differences between the several villages. Despite the fact that all Hopis shared a language and, with very few exceptions, shared fundamentally similar beliefs, practices, and rituals, as well as being organized in matrilineal kin groups with matrilocal residence, there was no overall "tribal" organization or even any formal mechanism for maintaining any inter-village cooperation. In fact, jealousy, suspicion, and latent hostility was typical of inter-village relationships. Even within a given village, interclan relationships were often strained; and it was almost inconceivable that intervillage coordination could ever be durable or genuine. According to Connelly (1979:539),

> Efforts to gain "tribal" unity among the Hopi relate to Hopi social organization only as a contemporary issue, following the enactment of the Indian Reorganization Act of 1934. The problems that attended the efforts to achieve Hopi political unity show that such unity was not encompassed within the traditional social structure and throw some light on why such a perception of unity was antithetical to Hopi culture.

Titiev made the point even more succinctly: "never has a leader arisen to mould the autonomous villages into a co-ordinated unit worthy of being called a Tribe" (1944:68).

The Indian Reorganization Act and Collier's "Indian New Deal" were of questionable value to any society which, like the Hopis and Tewas, had a long tradition of local, village autonomy; and the history of the Hopi "tribe" since 1934 provides ample evidence of the incompatibility of the act with Hopi political institutions.

In retrospect, it is clear that Collier, either failing to consider or choosing to ignore the pattern of local autonomy, sought to impose an antithetical structure on the Hopis by using his influence with the "friendly" Hopis and Tewas of First Mesa. It is not difficult to understand how he might have let himself be guided by the educated, English-speaking progressives whose educational background and political orientation predisposed them to welcome Collier's well intentioned, though very naive, promises of reform. His attempts to impose the terms of the Indian Reorganization Act on the Hopis cannot be justified on the basis of well-intentioned naivete or misguided idealism, however. Collier's letter of November 20, 1933, addressed to professional anthropologists, and his letter of January 20, 1934, to the Hopis, express the concern that a consolidation of political power might in the end, be troublesome for the Hopis. He was in receipt of reliable, current, expert testimony from Fred Eggan, who spent three months doing field research among the Hopis for Collier. Eggan's letter of January 11, 1934 to John Collier included an outline of Hopi social organization and explained that each village was autonomous and governed by its own hierarchy of native priests. The letter went on to explain that land was held by individual clans within each village and that the villages were strong and viable political entities that were, in Eggan's opinion, "entirely competent" to assume the responsibilities of self-government (Eggan 1934).

This expert testimony was confirmed by a letter from the *kikmongwi* [village chief] of Shongopavi to Collier dated March 4, 1934:

> In reply to your letter of January 20, 1934, regarding the matter as in forming or organizing a self-government, which we already have that has been handed down from generation to generation up to this time.

Even the Hopi agency superintendent suggested that reorganization could be carried out at the village level, where the *kikmongwi* would be "ready and willing to accept as much self-government as can be given them" (Hammond 1934). Had Collier been sincere in his professed desire to make the Bureau sensitive to the particular needs of different Indian societies, he might have been expected to profit from the advice which he, himself, had solicited from Eggan, from the *kikmongwi* of Shongopavi, and from his own agency superintendent, all of whom opposed the plan to organize a Hopi tribe.

The Hopi Tribe was organized, nonetheless; and the first step in its organization was a referendum on the issue of whether to adopt the general provisions of the act. This took place on June 15, 1935. Although demographic data on the Hopis and Tewas of the 1930s are difficult to obtain and interpret, it appears that some 40% of the Hopis and Tewas voted and 27% cast their votes in favor of adoption. To what extent those favoring adoption were aware of the implications of their vote is difficult to ascertain; but the results of this referendum were interpreted by Collier as a "big vote" in favor of his reforms.

Ratification of the constitution and the creation of a tribal council were to take place in 1936. Collier, himself, attended a preliminary meeting at Oraibi on April 4 of that year. Alexander Hutton, then superintendent of the Hopi Agency, admonished those present at the start of the meeting that they should 'confine [themselves] to something of benefit to all the Hopi people, and not just little petty grievances" (Collier 1936). Thus the agent established firm control at the start of what was supposed to have been a meeting for both Anglos and Indians to present their views. Collier spoke, admitting forthrightly that, on the basis of information he had received from anthropologists and from representatives of certain of the Hopi villages, he considered reorganization of a Hopi tribe a difficult problem. "I have not known what to do, and

I don't pretend that I know today just how to go about it," he said (Collier 1936). He went on to persuade those present that he was sensitive to their traditional social structure and then offered the opinion that the "time is at hand . . . to organize" (Collier 1936). If the Hopis and Tewas did not adopt a constitution and form a council, there would be grave consequences: they would be ineligible, for example, for the loan fund allocated by Congress for social services and economic support for the depression-stricken Hopis. Collier's actual words were: "The tribes who do organize and get their charter are the ones who get the money . . ." (Collier 1936). In addition to this economic argument he used a political one: Secretary of the Interior Ickes, President Roosevelt, and Collier, himself, might not be in power in another year; and "you don't know what the next President and the next Commissioner might do" (Collier 1936). Thus both economic and political arguments were used to persuade the meeting that the Hopi "Tribe" should organize itself without delay.

Collier also made assurances, however, that Hopi traditions would not be destroyed by the new program. Each individual village could "maintain its identity and freedom" at the same time that it joined others in a federation represented by a tribal council. The council would negotiate with the Bureau on behalf of all the Hopis and thus all would benefit from the opportunities for self-government offered by the act. A constitution would limit the council's power over the several villages and ensure that the internal affairs of each village would be the exclusive province of the local kikmongwi. In any event, the council would not come into being unless and until the Hopis, themselves, so desired.

The composition of the meeting cannot, of course, be ascertained at this late date. The "hostiles" doubtless stayed away in droves. We know something about the first speaker, however. This was a Baptist named Byron Adams, whose family has been mentioned earlier in connection with the early Christian converts of Second Mesa. Not surprisingly, Adams was enthusiastic about the new government policy and urged the meeting to adopt the Collier plan which would restore a proper, bilateral relationship between the Hopis and the Whites. He closed with the following statement:

> We have heard at first hand his plans and, it is our duty as Indians and as men to be true to each other and to back up this policy and to unite into an organization in order to work forward to an end so that we may take advantage of the Wheeler-Howard Act which is before us (Collier 1936).

The next speaker was Otto Lomavitu, a Christian interpreter for the Mennonite Church, who later became the first chairman of the Hopi Tribal Council. Lomavitu expressed his thanks to the Commissioner for coming out to Oraibi and his gratitude for the opportunities made possible by the Indian Reorganization Act. The plan, he said, would be another "way out whereby a poor Hopi could be given another start in life . . . (Collier 1936).

Another man who spoke in support of Collier's proposal was Tom Pavatea, a Tewa from First Mesa who, in 1894, established "what may have been the first Indian-operated store in the Southwest . . . a trading post at Polacca"

(Dockstader 1979:527). According to Edward Kennard (1979:559) he left an estate of more than $40,000 when he died in 1941. Pavatea supported the Collier proposal because the act guaranteed "the Hopi the freedom to enjoy life" (Collier 1936).

It would seem that those who attended the meeting, and especially those who spoke, were self-selected assimilationists, predisposed or already committed to the American road. At any rate Collier returned to Washington with what he interpreted to be a mandate from the Hopi "Tribe." Before leaving Oraibi, however, he assured the Hopis that each of the several villages would retain its identity and freedom, that the Council would not be empowered to interfere in local affairs, and that a sensitive and experienced agent would be sent to assist the Hopis and Tewas in drawing up a constitution that would reflect the views of all parties concerned. It seemed that, at last, Violet Pooleyama's dream of "a good man, a kind man who understands the Hopi people" might come true. But within the next six months all three of Collier's promises were broken.

The agent chosen to assist the Hopis in making their decisions relative to the implementation of the Indian Reorganization Act was Oliver La Farge, who had been educated at Groton and Harvard (where he received an M.A. in anthropology in 1929) and was well known for *Laughing Boy*, a romantic novel set in the Southwest for which he had won a Pulitzer Prize. He was not the unbiased and solicitous agent that Collier had promised though. It soon became evident that he was a committed advocate for reorganizing the Hopis as a tribe.

La Farge noted a number of "unpleasant Hopi characteristics" which he attributed to the "hostile" faction, whose members, he said, were "mean spirited" Indians whose "materialism, self-seeking, smugness, and quarrelsomeness" left them "cantankerous and tight-minded" (Indian Law Resource Center 1979:35–36). Even more vexing to him was their total disregard for cleanliness:

> The contrast between the dirt at Mishongnavi and the cleanness of the meal I'd eaten [at a Tewa's house on First Mesa] was startling. Even though the latter was also off the floor. When I got home I washed and gargled with Zionite (Indian Law Resource Center 1979:33).

Like the many missionaries and government agents that preceeded him, La Farge found the Tewas of First Mesa superior to the conservative Hopis. They were "cleaner, less pronounced in smell, and more forthright" than the Hopis. Moreover, they were "not afraid of fighting," while the Hopis had a "cult of peace which reaches an extreme" (Indian Law Resource Center 1979:34). One could scarcely find more convincing evidence for his partisanship than this description, for in La Farge's view the Hopis were both too peaceful and too "cantankerous." He distinguished, however, between friendly, progressive Hopis and hostile, conservative ones. He encountered the former in a village on First Mesa where,

> Due to the influence of the Tewas, and considerable intermixture with the Navajos, this village shows the least of the unpleasant Hopi characteristics

53

. . . it is the most accustomed to contact with the government, and in general the easiest to deal with (Indian Law Resource Center 1979:35).

La Farge also approved of the "friendlies" of Bacabi, who had sided with the "hostiles" in 1906, then repented and, when they were not readmitted to Oraibi, had established the village of Bacabi nearby (Dockstader 1979:529). This too was a "clean" village, inhabited by "progressives":

Consciously progressive and with a self made chief who believes in cooperation with the Government, they have formed an extremely pleasant little group. In contrast to the filth of other villages, this one is proud of its cleanliness, and will compare in appearance to the Rio Grande Pueblos (Indian Law Resource Center 1979:39).

THE HOPI CONSTITUTION

On August 28, 1936, La Farge sent a constitution to Collier for his approval before presenting it to the Hopis for a final vote. In the accompanying letter he wrote that the document had been revised many times to accommodate the wishes of the different villages and that both traditionals and progressives had accepted the document (La Farge 1936). Both these assertions were, at best, misleading. He had travelled 5100 miles back and forth between the villages in an attempt to present the document to the Hopis; but the hearings were rarely attended by more than a small fraction of the village population. Moreover, La Farge was well aware of the determined opposition which he had encountered from Dan Katchongva, the *kikmongwi* of Hotevilla, and so could scarcely have believed that the traditionals supported the document. It was La Farge, himself, the Hopis and Tewas of First Mesa, and the progressives of Third Mesa that embraced the constitution and were largely responsible for its language.

The preamble states that the constitution is adopted by the self-governing Hopi and Tewa villages of Arizona to provide a way of working together for peace and agreement between the villages, and of preserving the good things of Hopi life and to provide a way of organizing to deal with the United States Government and the outside world generally.

I will not review the entire document here, but certain provisions are of particular relevance to the issue of local autonomy vs. centralized rule.

Article I states that the Council's jurisdiction extends to all Hopi villages and that the Council is authorized to represent the Hopi Tribe in negotiating with all outside parties.

Article II defines membership in terms of matrilineal descent and reserves to the *kikmongwi* of each village the power to accept or reject non-members who marry into the village.

Article III declares that the Hopi Tribe is a federation consisting of nine "villages": First Mesa (which includes Walpi, Sichomovi, and Hano), Mishongnovi, Shipaulovi, Shongopavi, Oraibi, New Oraibi, Bacabi, Hotevilla, and Moenkopi.

Article IV pertains to representation in the Council. The number of representatives from each of the nine constituent villages is to be determined by population; and all representatives must be recognized by their several *kikmongwi*. No business is to be conducted without a quorum, which consists of representatives from five or more of the nine villages.

Article V contains procedures for the impeachment of Council members accused of crimes or of neglecting their official duties.

Article VI enumerates the powers of the Council, which include the power:

to represent and speak for the Hopi Tribe in all matters for the welfare of the tribe, and to negotiate with the federal, state, and local governments, and with the councils of other tribes.

to employ lawyers, the choice of lawyers and fining of fees to be subject to the approval of the Secretary of Interior.

to prevent the sale, disposition, lease, or encumberance of tribal lands, or other tribal property.

Article VI also empowered the Council to manage and expend tribal funds, to make ordinances and administer justice in tribal courts, and to regulate the activities of the tribal business organization. Of particular relevance in the present context was a provision that empowered the Council "to protect the arts, crafts, traditions, and ceremonies of the Hopi Indians."

Section 3 of Article VI is of particular interest when we recall the assurance given by Collier in April, 1936 that each village would "maintain its freedom and identity" (Collier 1936). It provides that the Council

may exercise such further powers as may in the future be delegated to it by members of the tribe or by the Secretary of the Interior, or any duly authorized official or agency of the state or federal government.

No provision was made to restrict these broad powers or to prevent them from infringing upon those of "the self-governing Hopi and Tewa villages" mentioned in the preamble.

Article VII provides that land is to remain under the control of the clans, except for certain "range land" which is to be supervised by the Council—another instance of the ambiguous wedding of local autonomy with council rule.

Article IX states that all members of the tribe are to share in the economic success of the Tribe and that the general provisions of the First Amendment to the Constitution of the United States (freedom of religion, speech, press, and assembly) will apply on the reservation.

Finally Article X specifies procedures for amending the constitution.

Collier returned the constitution with minor changes; and, after La Farge's departure, the local agents were left to arrange for a referendum on ratification of the constitution, which took place on October 26, 1936. There were 650 votes for ratification, 104 against, a turnout of more than 47%, if one believes Collier's population estimate of 1600 Hopis and Tewas. Haas' *Ten Years of Tribal Government Under the I.R.A.*, a 1947 publication of the Department of the Interior, gives the population for the year 1935 as 2,538, but also indicates that the population in 1936 was 3,444, more than twice Collier's figure. Richard Clemmer has suggested a way to reconcile these discrepant figures by assuming that

> 3,444 must be the total population, and 2,538 perhaps the adult population. . . . And 754 people voting in the 1936 constitutional referendum does not constitute 50 percent of the eligible voters flocking to the polls. It represents 29 percent (Clemmer 1978:60–61, as quoted in Indian Law Resource Center 1979:53).

If Clemmer's analysis is correct, the voting turnout was not sufficient to ratify the constitution. A year earlier Congress had specified that a turnout of 30% of the adult population was required to become a tribe under the terms of the Indian Reorganization Act. In any event, there can be no question that many Hopis registered their disapproval by staying away from the polls. At Hotevilla, for example, a "Hostile" stronghold since 1906, 13 of the 250 eligible voters went to the polls.

Another feature of this referendum casts doubt on the intent of those who actually did mark their ballots, which had been designed by La Farge before his departure in August. The "X" for rejection and the circle for adoption may well have been intended by some voters to be interpreted quite otherwise. One voter told Clemmer that

> . . . since the circle and cross are well known in Hopi symbology, having certain meanings in the Hopi point of view, some who voted thought the white people had the same meanings and were therefore confident in using those same marks (Clemmer 1977:13).

A letter from Allen G. Harper, a field administrator, to A. G. Hutton, superintendent of the Hopi Agency, indicates that La Farge was aware that the design of the ballot might cause confusion as to how to vote for or against adoption. The letter goes on, however, to state that La Farge "thinks that the vote might be adversely affected if a change is made" (Harper 1936). Perhaps for this reason the ballot was not changed. All things considered, the referendum can scarcely be said to have fulfilled Collier's assurances, given in April. According to the Indian Law Resource Center (1979:52), "it might at best be characterized as wholesale manipulation and deception. At worst it might fairly be characterized as a fraud."

The Hopi Constitution, Council, and "Tribe" were all destined to fail. Collier, himself, was constrained to write, long after, that

> The Hopis adopted this constitution and it has never worked. The constitution conformed to the institutional structures of the Hopis, but it assumed . . . that the Hopis would utilize the constitution with what may be termed an Occidental rationality (Collier 1963:218, as quoted in Indian Law Resource Center 1979:66).

CHAPTER 5

THE HOPIS AND THE TEWAS

The Melvilles, and most subsequent visitors to the Hopi Reservation, have perceived the Hopis as "isolated." Their isolation stems, however, not only from their geographic position in a remote corner of the desert Southwest. They are completely surrounded by the vast Navajo Reservation, which acts as a social, as well as a geographic, buffer between the Hopis and the American Road. But this is not all. The Indian residents of the Hopi Reservation themselves consist of two very different ethnic groups, one of which, the Tewas, has traditionally acted as a buffer between the Hopis and the outside world. One can scarcely understand "Hopi" participation in the tourist business and the Indian art business or "Hopi" relationships with missionaries, schools, the federal government, and certain corporations which extract mineral resources from the reservation under the terms of leases negotiated with the "Hopi Tribe" without some awareness of the history of ethnic relationships on the Hopi Mesas. Hopi history, Hopi art, Hopi economics, and certainly Hopi politics can only be understood in the context of the ethnic composition of the "Hopi Tribe." The Hopis, whose ancestors occupied the area before the Spanish *entrada*, have values, expectations, institutions and understandings, all of which differentiate them from the Tewas, whose ancestors emigrated from the Rio Grande in the seventeenth century.

The events leading up to this Tewa migration have been succinctly described by the late Edward P. Dozier, who was both a professional anthropologist, who studied the Arizona Tewas for a number of years, and a native Tewa speaker, born and raised in Santa Clara Pueblo, a Tewa community in New Mexico. Dozier's account is as follows:

> The ancestors of the Hopi have been residents of the mesa-top villages for many centuries, but the Tewa are newcomers; they are the descendants of refugees from New Mexico who fled from Spanish oppression in the seventeenth century. The coming of the Spaniards was a major catastrophe to the peaceful Pueblo Indians residing along the Rio Grande and its tributaries in New Mexico. White man's diseases and the fanatical pogroms of the Spaniards to Christianize and "civilize" the Indians took a large toll of Pueblo lives. Many of these Indians fled their villages and joined the nomadic Apaches, while others sought refuge among the sedentary Hopi.

> First Mesa, the easternmost escarpment of the Hopi Mesas, contains three villages: one of them is the Tewa community of Hano; the other two villages are Hopi. Further west on similar mesa-tops are other Hopi villages; only First Mesa, however, harbors a community different in speech and customs from the others (Dozier 1966:1).

It should be noted here that, while the Tewa village is the only culturally and linguistically deviant village on the Hopi Mesas, its role as the peripheral "guard" village for First Mesa has parallels on the other mesas. According to Fred Eggan, "The Hopi model for their society centers on a traditional 'mother' village, a 'colony' village, and a 'guard' or protector village, and this pattern is repeated on most of the mesas" (1966:124).

The ancestors of the Arizona Tewas were called "Tanos" or "Thanos" by the seventeenth century Spaniards. They were enthusiastic participants in the Pueblo Rebellion of 1680. Indeed, 300 of them were killed in the siege of Santa Fe, where 47 others were captured and executed (Dozier 1966:9). They and the other pueblo peoples succeeded, however, in driving the Spaniards back into Mexico. When De Vargas regained control of the pueblos in 1693, the Thanos were either enslaved or "dispersed among some of the more peaceful pueblos in order to quell their rebellious nature" (Dozier 1966:3, 11). Resettlement on Spanish terms was evidently not acceptable to the Thanos, however. They rose with certain other pueblos in 1696; and, when this revolt collapsed, they fled, first to Jemez Pueblo and later to the Hopi country. According to Stanislawski, they did not arrive among the Hopis until shortly after the destruction of Awatovi, a Christian Hopi village which was destroyed by conservatives from other Hopi villages in November, 1700. Stanislawski writes that the Hopis "would presumably have been delighted to have a new guard village at the head of the trail, particularly after their attack on Awatovi, which they no doubt expected would be avenged" (1979:600). In any event, the Thanos, that is the ancestors of the present Arizona Tewas, were allocated land by the Hopis. According to Stanislawski, citing Fewkes (1899:256–259; 1900:614–616) and Mindeleff (1891:36), they "may have first built a village near Coyote Spring at the south foot of the present entrance road to Tewa Village, but after defeating the Utes in a battle north of the gap, they were granted permanent farmlands by the Hopi, and their present mesa-top village site" (1979:600).

The Tewa immigrants were not a disorganized and routed band of refugees from the Spanish Terror; they were a well disciplined and fiercely independent people who had fought bravely and with considerable success in two rebellions and who were prudent enough to sacrifice their homeland in return for a secure refuge on a defensible site well removed from the seat of Spanish power. They had their own language, rituals and political organization and were not at all interested in assimilating into Hopi society. Their concern was to establish themselves in a secure position where they could maintain their own autonomy and their own ethnic identity free from alien interference.

According to Tewa oral tradition, the Thanos were invited to resettle among the Hopis and were given, as the site for their new village, the area at the top of the trail up First Mesa so that they might be the first to engage invading forces, specifically the Utes and Paiutes. We know of at least one instance in which they, or their presence, assisted in defending the Hopis against a Spanish military force as well. Narvaez Valverde's account of the Spaniards' rather ineffectual response to the destruction of Awatovi, their only Christian bastion in the Hopi country, is as follows:

At this time, his people being infuriated because the Indians of the pueblo of Aguatubi [Awatovi] had been reduced to our holy faith and the obedience of our king, he [Espeleta, the chief of Oraibi] came with more than one hundred of his people to the said pueblo, entered it, killed all the braves, and carried off the women, leaving the pueblo to this day desolate and unpeopled. Learning of this outrage, Governor Don Pedro Rodriguez Cubero made ready some soldiers to punish it, and in the following year of 1701 went to the said province of Moqui [Hopi], taking with him the aforesaid religious, Fray Juan Caricochea and Fray Antonio Miranda. With his armed force he killed some Indians and captured others, but not being very well prepared to face the multitudes of the enemy, he withdrew and returned without being able to reduce them, especially as the Moquis had with them the Tanos Indians, who, after committing outrages had taken refuge among them and had risen at their command (Narvaez Valverde 1937:386, as quoted in Dozier 1966:14).

In 1716 an army of Spaniards and their Indian allies attempted to return the Tewas to Christendom. The Spanish commander, Govenor Felix Martinez

. . . explained to them the sole purpose for which [he] had come with the army, that is, that they should offer submission to the Divine and human Majesty and bring back all of the Indians who had rebelled, some in the year '80 [1680] and others in '96; that they should return to their own pueblos whence they fled. . . . (Bloom 1931:204–205, as quoted in Dozier 1966:14).

When the Tewas declined to submit, Martinez opened fire, killing 8 and wounding many others. He then proposed to the Hopis of First Mesa that they permit him to ascend and take the Tewas prisoner. According to Martinez' account, the cacique of Walpi announced that the Hopis of Walpi, on First Mesa,

were already friends with the Spaniards and did not desire the friendship of the said Thanos; that they will be severely punished for the harm they have done in making war . . . that many of their people had been killed and wounded through the fault of the said Thanos. . . . (Bloom 1931:218, as quoted in Dozier 1966:14).

The Spaniards, despite assurances from Walpi that they might climb the mesa without fear of attack by the Hopis, thought it best to remain below, fearing, no doubt, a vigorous Tewa defense, aided perhaps by Walpi duplicity. In any event, Martinez merely destroyed the Tewa crops and livestock and returned to Santa Fe.

The seventeenth century Tewa refugees did not become integrated into Hopi social and ceremonial life. They and their descendants were given undesirable cropland, a relatively undesirable site for their village, and inferior social status. Dozier describes the history of social relations between the Hopis and Tewas of First Mesa as follows:

The traditions of the Hopi and the Tewa indicate that the community of Hano remained in a minority status for a long time. Tewa inhabitants were denied full participation in Hopi ceremonies, and only the poorer plots of land were made available for them to farm. Hano, in return, clung tenaciously to its own cultural forms and carefully prevented the diffusion of its language and customs to its neighbors (Dozier 1966:1).

The Tewa Village is the most recently occupied of the three villages on First Mesa. The Tewa immigrants were poor, few in number, and, because of their recent history, war-like. They also spoke a strange language and, from the Hopi point of view, practiced barbarous customs. It is virtually certain, for example, that the first generation of Tewa immigrants lacked a matrilineal kinship system, which is the cornerstone of Hopi social organization. Their rituals and religious beliefs were, no doubt, similar to those of the Hopis; but their emphasis on curing rituals, rather than weather control, must have made their religious beliefs and practices appear to orthodox Hopis as, at best, deviant and, at worst, perverted travesties of the eternal truths of Hopi orthodoxy. It is not surprising, therefore, that the Tewas were discriminated against. Stanislawski, citing Dozier (1954:289–291; 1966:23–26), reports that "Rules against intermarriage with Tewa were strictly enforced by the Hopi during the eighteenth and early nineteenth centuries" (1979:590). Discrimination is also indicated by the Tewa oral tradition, which has been recounted annually, as a part of the Winter Solstice Ceremony, to every generation of Tewas since their resettlement in the seventeenth century. The myth may have exaggerated the severity of this discrimination; it is, after all, a partisan account. It is worthy of careful consideration mainly because every individual born to a Tewa mother since the seventeenth century has been taught the myth and the values and beliefs that are implicit in it. It is important also, because the myth may well be the chief mechanism by which the Tewas preserved their ethnic identity and their social boundaries until they were in a position to overcome the intolerance of the Hopis. For this reason, the myth and its role in Tewa-Hopi social history may have implications for contemporary Americans still casting about for ways to make "equality of opportunity" a reality.

The Tewa migration myth describes the migration to First Mesa as a charitable service rendered in response to pleas by the Hopis for protection from their enemies.

> Four times the Walpi Bear Clan Chief and Snake Clan Chief [Hopi clans on First Mesa] came to our village at *Tsawadeh* [former home of the Southern Tewa in New Mexico]. They brought with them prayer sticks that represented the things that would be given to us if we would come and fight their enemies. There was one for the women that were promised to our men; there was one for the village site that we would occupy; there was one for the springs from which we would obtain our drinking water; there was one for the land on which we could raise our corn and other crops. . . . They drew for us on the sand the large stalks of corn that were raised on the land that would be ours. They extended both arms to indicate the size of the ears of corn that grew on this land. "All this will be yours if you will come and live among us as our protectors," they said. "In our land you will have plenty to eat and your storehouses will always be full" (Dozier 1966:17).

The migration myth makes no mention of Spanish oppression in the old homeland, but stresses the unfair and inhospitable treatment which the Tewas received from the Hopis after settling at Hano. Thus the seventeenth century Tewas' desperate need for a safe haven from the Spaniards has been forgotten. What remains is a dramatic contrast between the morally and ritually degenerate and politically perfidious Hopis and the stalwart, charitable, and honorable Tewas.

> How pitifully ignorant must have been our ancestors to believe the Hopi! Little did they know that they would be so miserably deceived. . . . Our grandmothers and grandfathers were not permitted to ascend the mesa when they arrived at Hopi, but were forced to make camp below. When some of them petitioned Walpi women for food, they were told to cup their hands to receive a corn-meal gruel and boiling hot, it was poured into their hands. When the Tewas let the gruel slip to the ground and proceeded to nurse their burnt hands, the Hopi women laughed and berated them for being weak and soft.

> . . . When our ancestors had defeated the Utes and made life safe for the Hopi, they asked for the land, women, and food which had been promised to them. But the Hopis refused to give them these things. Then it was that our poor ancestors had to live like beasts, foraging on the wild plants and barely subsisting on the meager supply of food. Our ancestors lived miserably, beset by disease and starvation. The Hopi, well fed and healthy, laughed and made fun of our ancestors (Dozier 1966:18).

The myth relates that the Tewas successfully repelled repeated attacks on the Hopi villages and, by so doing, gained such a reputation as warriors that the enemy raids ceased altogether. They did not gain favor, however, with the Hopis; and so the Tewa chiefs determined to lay a curse upon them.

> Our clan chiefs dug a pit between Hano and the Hopi villages [on First Mesa] and told the Hopi clan chiefs to spit into it. When they had all spat, our clan chiefs spat above the spittle of the Hopi. The pit was refilled, and then our clan chiefs declared:

> "Because you behaved in a manner unbecoming to human beings, we have sealed knowledge of our language and our way of life from you. You and your descendants will never learn our language and our ceremonies, but we will learn yours. We will ridicule you in both your language and our own" (Dozier 1966:18).

The curse on the Hopis has proved to be a self-fulfilling prophecy. It is significant that "The Hopi believe in the consequences of the curse as strongly as the Tewa" (Dozier 1966:19). Initially, no doubt, the curse was effective because it merely sanctioned what was already established practice. The Hopis had no incentive to learn the language or rituals of a despised minority; but the Tewas had every reason to learn the language and practices of the dominant majority. The effect of the curse was to sanction Tewa acquisition of the Hopi language and culture without compromising Tewa identity and without obscuring the social boundaries that separated the two groups. The Tewas adopted the Hopi matrilineal kinship system and the Hopi pattern of matrilocal residence and promptly used them to maintain their ethnic solidarity.

As Fred Eggan put it, "... the Tewa have maintained their social identity and language, in the face of growing intermarriage with the Hopi, by a strict observance of matrilocal residence" (1966:124). Tewa women all resided at the Tewa village, in accordance with the Hopi custom of matrilocal residence whereby husbands move in with the relatives of their wives. This ensured that all children of Tewa women were brought up in a Tewa speaking community. By the latter part of the nineteenth century, however, the Tewa men were free to marry either Tewas or Hopis. In the latter case, they lived in the Hopi villages, again in accordance with the Hopi residence pattern; and their children were brought up in Hopi speaking communities. Some Hopi men, of course, married Tewa women and had Tewa children at Hano. These Hopi husbands and fathers, however, were invariably addressed in the Hopi language; and, if they made occasional efforts to respond in Tewa, these awkward attempts were taken as empirical evidence of the viability of the curse—everyone knows that Hopis can never learn to speak Tewa. Thus by adapting certain aspects of Hopi culture, specifically the kinship, marriage, and residence rules, the Tewas, paradoxically, ensured their own persistence as a discrete and bounded ethnic group.

The curse and its social consequences have several important aspects. The curse predicts and acts as a charter for assymetrical acculturation, thus making a virtue of necessity by successfully predicting the inevitable. But it also regulates the inevitable by providing for specific and limited social and linguistic changes, however sweeping these may have been. The curse provides that the Tewas will learn Hopi, for example; but also that they will not forget Tewa and that the Hopis will not learn Tewa, so that Tewas will always be able to communicate in a code that is, or is believed to be, entirely opaque to the Hopis. The curse makes no provision for Tewa adoption of the Hopi clan system, but when the practice of reckoning descent through the female line was adopted, it ensured that, since Tewas, like Hopis, must be members of their mothers' clans, no Tewa would ever become a member of a Hopi clan, nor could any Hopi ever be a member of a Tewa clan. Likewise, when the Tewas adopted Hopi residence rules, this accommodation to Hopi norms served only to maintain the social boundary between the ethnic groups, for matrilocal residence ensures that all the children of Tewa clans will grow up in bilingual, Tewa households and that all the children of Hopi clans will grow up in monolingual, Hopi households, regardless of who their fathers may be.

The frequent recitation of the curse in the Kiva and in Tewa homes, as part of the migration myth, ensured selective and regulated social interaction with the Hopis within well defined social boundaries. It also served as a bottomless well of self-esteem for a people who might otherwise have sought to abandon their lowly social status by assimilating into Hopi society. The myth has served for almost three centuries to maintain the Tewas as a clearly bounded ethnic group, capable of adapting to changed conditions, and secure in the knowledge that the prophecy of their old chiefs is still binding on Hopis as well as Tewas, as anyone can verify for himself simply by speaking Tewa to a Hopi.

By the middle of the twentieth century, when Dozier did his fieldwork, however, the social and cultural boundaries between the Tewas and the Hopis of First Mesa were beginning to break down.

> It is clear at present that the attitudes of hostility and antagonism . . . are being ameliorated. For example, resistance to the Hopi way of life is stronger with the older Tewa. At the Winter Solstice ceremony it is old men who emphasize that the Tewa must not forget Hopi injustices. Young people have much in common with the Hopi, and they tend to minimize and even laugh off these serious admonitions. Consequently, old legends tend to disappear with the passing of the aged, and young Tewa seem content to forget them. Reduced friction between the two groups in recent years seems to be directly related to white contact. The unfavorable position of the Tewa on First Mesa induced them to cooperate more readily with whites. As a result of this cooperation the Tewa became acquainted with the techniques of livestock raising and wage work. The revival of pottery making, as we have noted, started at Hano and diffused to the Hopi. Tewa successes with these new economic activities brought about reduced tensions and emulation from their Hopi neighbors on First Mesa, which in turn paved the way to greater interdependence and cooperation, particularly in social and secular activities (Dozier 1966:29–30).

The gradual obliteration of ethnic distinctions in the present century, resulting from Hopi emulation of the Tewas rather than Tewa emulation of the Hopis, can only be understood in the context of twentieth century American intervention. Dozier's reconstruction of the history of ethnic relationships on First Mesa is useful in this connection:

> The original Tewa group came into the profoundly religiously oriented Hopi society. The Tewa religious repertoire was less complex than the Hopi and it emphasized curing . . . rather than weather "control." Tewa religion was also more secular because of a politically oriented social organization . . . and a hundred years of Spanish influence. As newcomers, the Tewas were assigned the role of "protectors" in the traditional Hopi manner. To a religion concerned primarily with "weather control" through ritual the Tewa had little to contribute. Their curing societies may have been welcome, but they probably had no important ceremonies to appease the harsh environment. Skill as warriors was helpful, but war was despicable to the Hopi and was not a prestige-bearing activity. If the Tewa displayed the outgoing, aggressive personalities that characterize their present descendants, they were probably even less desired, for Hopi behavior is ideally passive.
>
> Tewa values at Hopi must have taken literally a "back seat." The Hopi no doubt had little respect for this religiously poverty-stricken society. They did "use" the ancestors of the Tewa, however, in the roles that they disdained—the prestigeless position of warriors, and later as interpreters and go-betweens. In an attempt to assert their own self-importance, the Tewa accused the Hopi of inhospitality and ungracious behavior. They bolstered their own group ego by remaining aloof, reiterating Hopi injustices, and extolling their own virtues as warriors and emissaries (Dozier 1966:30).

We have already made the case for the effectiveness of Tewa military activity in the Hopi interest. There is also documentary evidence for their effectiveness as diplomats in the service of the Hopis. Thus James C. Calhoun, the first U.S. Indian agent for the Territory of New Mexico, received a delegation of Hopis in 1850 who inquired into the "purposes and views of the government of the United States towards them" (Calhoun 1915, letter no. 82, as quoted in Dozier 1966:15). Calhoun reported that their leader, whom he referred to as the "Cacique of all the [Hopi] Pueblos," was a Tewa from Hano. Twelve years later Beadle found that the chief of Walpi communicated with outsiders through a Tewa interpreter or speaker, "a tall old fellow with a merry twinkle in his eye," named Misiamtewah who "had visited the Mormon settlements and Santa Fe, and could speak Spanish, Moqui [Hopi], Tegua and a little English and Navajo, besides being fluent in the sign language" (Beadle 1878:266–267, as quoted in Dozier 1966:27).

In the late nineteenth century Tom Polacca, another Tewa, who was a brother of Nampeyo, succeeded to the role of interpreter for the Hopis (Stanislawski 1979:588, fig. 1). Polacca "served as interpreter and speaker" and "learned to speak English and represented the Hopi in important conferences, accompanying in 1890 a delegation of Hopi chiefs to Washington, D.C. . . ." (Dozier 1966:27). In the early 1950s, when Dozier was doing field work on First Mesa, "the official Hopi interpreter was Albert Yava, a Tewa Indian" and on one occasion, when the superintendent of the agency arranged for a Hopi to act as interpreter at a meeting with Hopi chiefs, the Hopis "refused flatly to go on with the meeting unless the Tewa interpreter could be secured" (Dozier 1966:27). The Hopis, then, have a well established and long standing tradition of using Tewas as intermediaries in their interactions with outsiders, civil as well as military.

One of the roles which, being inconsistent with Hopi norms, has been assumed by the Tewas is that of policeman. Leo Crane, who was a Hopi agent in the second decade of this century, described the relative aptitude of Hopis and Tewas for policework:

> The Hopi do not make good policemen, and certainly not in a cohort of one. Their name implies "the peaceful ones." Their towns are ruled largely by pueblo opinion. If a resident acquires the reputation of being unreasonable and unfeeling, as a policeman often must, his standing in the outraged community may affect all other phases of his life. Therefore the Hopi is not likely to become a very zealous officer when operating alone. And too, the Hopi fear the Navajo, as it is said the Navajo fear the Ute, and are useless when removed from the neighborhood of their homes.

> But many years ago, when the Hopi were sorely pressed by nomad enemies and had not even the consolation of telling their woes to an Indian Agent, they sent emissaries to their cousins, the Pueblo Indians of what is now New Mexico, and begged for a colony of warriors to reside with them. In response to this plea, and looking for something to their advantage, in 1700 came a band of Tewa. . . . They built a village atop the First Mesa, now called Tewa or Hano, where their descendants live today. . . .

> The Hopi invited warriors, and the warriors have graduated into policemen, for one learns to police the Hopi districts, and even to discipline some of the Navajo, with Tewa officers. They are dependable and courageous,

even belligerant; that is to say, they will fight when it is necessary and, strange thing among desert Indians, with their fists, taking a delight in blacking the opponent's eye. But one has to learn that the Hopi as policemen are fine ceremonial dancers (Crane 1925:136–137, as quoted in Dozier 1966:27–28).

The Tewas have filled a variety of roles to which the Hopis are traditionally averse. As one Tewa told Dozier, "We are criticized and ridiculed for whatever we do so why not perform the work that needs to be done?" (Dozier 1966:28). Their performance of tasks involving aggressiveness and self-assertion has perhaps always been tolerated, if not actively supported, by the Tewa community. But in this century it has received support from the Americans as well, who

> endorse the outgoing personality characteristics of the Tewa. Government officials and whites generally have praised the "progressive" Tewa and pointed to them as models of the "proper attitude" Indians should have in the modern world (Dozier 1966:28).

It is not surprising then that Nampeyo, who is credited with the revival of Sikyatki Polychrome pottery, was a Tewa, or that her relatives, who became producers of Indian ceramic art and adopted the custom of signing their names on their pottery, were also Tewas. Nor should it come as a surprise that the First Mesa villages, especially Hano, were receptive to mission and government schools. The Tewas, and later First Mesa people in general, were the emissaries, the fearless travelers, the assertive achievers, the polyglots, intellectuals and statesmen of the "Hopi Tribe." Small wonder that the Melvilles were entertained by Christian Hopis and by Tewas, who, if they were not exactly Christian, were nonetheless "progressive" and dependable friends of missionary and agent alike. According to Stanislawski, "many [Tewa] homes in 1925 had some Christian pictures on the walls; however, few Hopi-Tewa are really serious about Anglo religion . . ." (1979:599).

As the twentieth century wore on, First Mesa became more and more a single community oriented toward Tewa and American values. Dozier put it this way:

> White American contact altered the value system in favor of the Tewa. Americans like the Tewa are "practical," and the aggressive and outgoing personality of the Tewa is remarkably "American." The Tewa readily and enthusiastically took to stock-raising, wage work and the white man's schools. Their children, already trained in two languages, learned English more quickly than the Hopis. Moreover, their greater motivation as a minority spurred them to excel in the classroom. In the process, the Hopi began to develop a new respect for the Tewa. The Tewa role as emissaries and interpreters to the white people grew in importance and prestige. Their value orientation, remarkably like that of the newcomers, no longer had to take a back seat. The Hopi saw that "it paid to be like the whites," and the Tewa were providing the lead to this new and positive achievement.

The Tewa have thus exerted considerable influence on First Mesa, which has diffused in weaker currents to other Hopi villages. Today there is constant interaction and cooperation between the two populations on First Mesa. Intermarriages and the acquisition of relatives on both sides have intricately related all of the people. The "healthy-social climate" and a generally cooperative atmosphere with the government and outsiders, noted on First Mesa by various investigators, is attributable largely to the Tewa (Dozier 1966:30–31).

The curse which sealed the Hopis off forever from all knowledge of the Tewa language and way of life was, of course, never intended to apply to Americans. The Tewa clan chiefs are no doubt aware, however, that American Indian agents, missionaries, and tourists who understand Tewa are in extremely short supply, so that the Americans, no less than the Hopis, may be doomed never to learn the Tewas' language or their ceremonies, while, curse or no curse, there is nothing whatever to stop the Tewas from ridiculing the Americans in Tewa or English, or for that matter Hopi.

CHAPTER 6

THE SIKYATKI REVIVAL

Although the prehistoric Sikyatki Polychrome pottery native to the Hopi area was copied in the 1890s, it was not until about 1900 that the new and distinctive "Sikyatki Revival Style" can be said to have crystalized. This new style, which flourished in the first four decades of the twentieth century, incorporated certain selected elements of prehistoric Sikyatki and Payupki designs together with layouts derived from Sikyatki bowl interiors, but it also maintained certain characteristics of nineteenth century Polacca Polychrome designs. While the new Sikyatki Revival Style was clearly influenced by Anglo American preferences as well as by Indian American antecedents, it was radically different from other Anglo and Indian art forms, not only with regard to design, but also in terms of its vessel forms and its use of space, line, and color.

The term "Sikyatki Revival Style" has become the standard name for the painted ceramics produced on the Hopi Reservation since about 1900. It is used by collectors, dealers, and scholars (Bartlett 1936, Colton 1938, Sikorski 1968, Stanislawski 1978, Wade and McChesney 1981). It is characterized by designs which are derived from Sikyatki Polychrome, a pottery type made from about AD 1375 to about 1625. Although some scholars have emphasized the fact that the Sikyatki Revival Style derived its vessel forms from Sikyatki Polychrome (Wade and McChesney 1981:455) or the fact that it borrowed its use of color from Sikyatki Polychrome (Sikorski 1968:22), all agree that it involved the revival of designs associated with Sikyatki Polychrome. The Sikyatki Revival Style revived specific design units and design layouts which had been used by prehistoric potters (Figure 3).

According to Wade and McChesney (1980:9), prehistoric Sikyatki designs were first copied around 1890. These first copies were made at the suggestion of the trader, Thomas V. Keam, who evidently thought that the prehistoric designs would increase the value and marketability of Hopi pottery, because of the growing interest in Southwestern antiquities at the time. His influence resulted in the copying of prehistoric designs and sometimes vessel shapes; but the pigment and slip (a coating of thin clay) were identical to those of the late nineteenth century local pottery known as Polacca Polychrome. Accordingly, the earliest of the Sikyatki Revival Style wares had the white, crackled slip diagnostic for Polacca Polychrome and thus were, essentially, Polacca Polychrome pieces with Sikyatki designs. Such pieces have been classified by Wade and McChesney (1981:455) as Polacca Polychrome, "Style D."

A number of ceramic pieces with just such Polacca Polychrome slips and

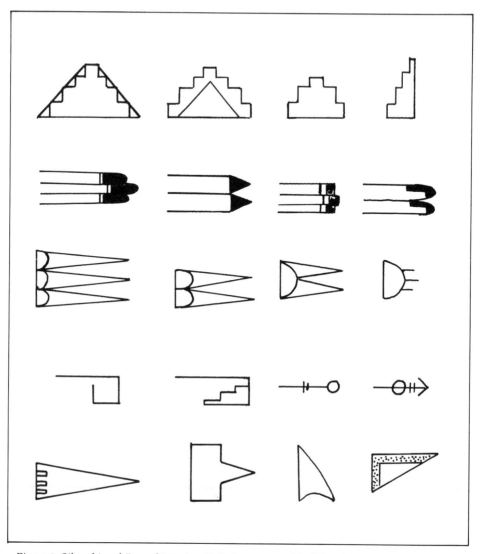

Figure 3. Sikyatki and Payupki Design Units Incorporated in Sikyatki Revival Style Designs

Sikyatki designs were obtained by the Museum of the American Indian, Heye Foundation, and the American Museum of Natural History in New York. Some of these were collected by George Pepper at the Tewa village on First Mesa in 1903–1904. Others, which are not dated, may be somewhat more recent, because Fewkes indicates that such items were being made as late as 1912:

> Much of the pottery offered for sale by Harvey and dealers in Indian objects along the Santa Fe Railroad in Arizona and New Mexico is imitation prehistoric Hopi ware made by Nampeo. The origin of this transformation was due partly to the author, who in the year named [1896] was excavating

the Sikyatki ruins and graves. Nampeo and her husband, Lesou, came to his camp, borrowed paper and pencil, and copied many of the ancient symbols found on the pottery vessels unearthed, and these she has reproduced on pottery of her own manufacture many times since that date. It is therefore necessary, at the very threshold of our study, to urge discrimination between modern and ancient pottery in the study of Hopi ware, and careful elimination of imitations. The modern pottery referred to is easily distinguished from the prehistoric, inasmuch as the modern is not made with as much care or attention to detail as the ancient. Also the surface of the modern pottery is coated with a thin slip which crackles in firing (Fewkes 1919:279).

Since there is no crackle on the surface of red-slipped, unslipped or self-slipped (slipped with the same clay from which the vessel was made) Sikyatki Revival wares, Fewkes can only be referring to Polacca Polychrome with Sikyatki designs, a kind of pottery that was clearly transitional between the earlier Polacca Polychrome and the later Sikyatki Revival Style wares.

This passage from Fewkes reveals something of the nature of Fewkes' relationship with Nampeyo. Later writers magnified the influence of Fewkes, which seems to have been restricted to the loan of paper and pencils. Frisbie (1973) has pointed out that Fewkes neither encouraged Nampeyo nor aided her in developing the new pottery style. Indeed, his primary concern was to see that her work should not be confused with prehistoric pottery. Thus he would have had more incentive to oppose her enterprise than to support it. On the other hand, Fewkes and his assistant may have indirectly encouraged Nampeyo in her experiments by voicing their admiration for prehistoric designs. Direct encouragement for copying these designs may have come from Keam, however, who must have recognized her ability as a potter. Alexander Stephen, who lived with Keam, wrote in 1892 that

The Walpi women alone understand well the art of pottery and its decorations. Hano women do make some pottery and decorate it, but it is not beautiful. I called their attention to Nûmpéyo, but they said she was the exception and had learned her art from the Hopi women (Stephen 1936:1020).

Nampeyo was, indeed, exceptional. Her earlier pieces were made with a Polacca Polychrome slip (Collins 1974:no. 9; Wade and McChesney 1981:455). But by 1903 she was making vessels that were either self-slipped or unslipped, like prehistoric Sikyatki Polychrome. According to Walter Hough, who was with Fewkes in 1896, Nampeyo not only copied designs from prehistoric pottery but "experimented with Sikyatki clays, matched the pigments used in decoration," and produced vessels that were "unslipped like the ancient ware" (Hough 1917:322). This suggests that Nampeyo may have abandoned the Polacca slip as early as 1896. Nampeyo was also important because she was the first Indian artist to be recognized by the American public. She was considered a producer of "art pottery" (see Chapter 3) and as such was monetarily compensated.

Although Nampeyo was clearly the central figure in the development of

Sikyatki Revival pottery, this style was quickly adopted by several of her Tewa and Hopi contemporaries on First Mesa who wished to participate in the American cash economy. When Mrs. Melville acquired Sikyatki Revival Style pieces in 1927 she took care to write the maker's name in pencil on the bottom of each piece. Thus we have not only a sample of Sikyatki Revival Style pottery acquired in 1927, but also a means of differentiating the pervasive characteristics of this style, as of 1927, from the idiosyncrasies of a number of individual craftsmen. The work of at least nine different Sikyatki Revival potters is represented in the Melville Collection.

A variety of Sikyatki Revival pottery shapes derived from Sikyatki Polychrome are represented in the Melville Collection (Figure 4). Two forms are

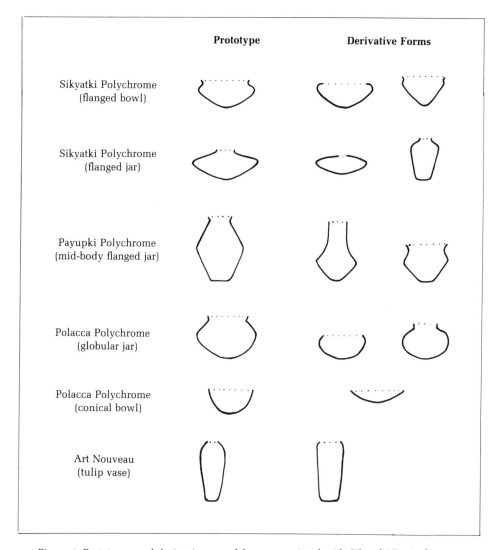

Figure 4. *Prototypes and derivative vessel forms associated with Sikyatki Revival wares*

related to the flanged Sikyatki Polychrome bowl: one is a similar shaped bowl, the other has an elongated body and, hence, is a jar. One potter, known to us only as "Lucy's mother", uses the shape or form of the prehistoric Sikyatki Polychrome bowl (page 77). The only other shape used by "Lucy's mother" was that of the derived bowl form (Plate 17).

Although the shape of the prehistoric, flanged Sikyatki Polychrome jar was commonly copied in the early 1900s, this was no longer the case in 1927. Apart from what might be a child's attempt at reproducing this form (Plate 12: lower left) there are no vessels of this shape in the Melville Collection. There are, however, two derivative forms. One is the same as the Sikyatki Polychrome jar except that it lacks the small neck of the prehistoric form and has a flat, rather than a rounded base (Plate 7). The most common shape that may be derived from the Sikyatki Polychrome jar is also similar to vases of Anglo manufacture. This form (Plates 8, 9) has a straight to out-flaring neck, shoulder, elongated vase body and flat base. It is possible, however, that this form was derived from vessels of Anglo manufacture, as were the "tulip" vase form and the related cylindrical vase form. In contrast to the tulip vase, which is always referred to as a "vase" in Hopi, these vessels have a native Hopi name, si·vɨ. This would indicate that, regardless of its origin, the Hopis themselves conceive of this form as native.

Excluding miniatures, there are more tulip vase form vessels in this collection than any other shape of vessel. This form has no Hopi or Tewa antecedent and seems to have been introduced about 1920. These vases (Plates 3, 18 and 19) are, in fact, copies of an Art Nouveau form which may have become known to the Hopi through mail order catalogues (Chapter 3). This shape was entirely foreign to Hopi and Tewa concepts of container categories; and, although these forms have been produced for sale for 60 years, they are still referred to by their makers as "vases", there being no Hopi term for them (Wyckoff n.d. chapter 4:2).

Quite different from the tulip vase form vessels is the vase or jar form derived from Payupki Polychrome. There are no vessels in the form of the Payupki Polychrome jar; and the three vessels (Plates 29, 33 and 35) in the Payupki derived jar and bowl forms were made by a single potter, Sellie. (See caption of Plate 29.) This woman was the only potter known to have decorated her vessels with an undulating snake band.

By 1927 the globular Polacca Polychrome jar form had been modified, a straight neck having replaced the everted neck used earlier. The globular bowl is also clearly derived from this Polacca Polychrome prototype. Over 50% of all the bowls in the Melville Collection are either conical bowls, also a common Polacca Polychrome form, or the derived flat bowls. All of Ruth Takala's bowls were conical (Plate 16). Her work is distinctive in several other respects: she alone used the Polacca Polychrome bird design (Plates 25 and 32); and all of her pieces are either of Polished Red Ware (Plates 16, 18 left, and 25 upper) or Red & White Ware (Plate 32 upper). Despite all this evidence for individual variation, however, most of the potters used a variety of shapes and alternated between a variety of wares. And it is significant that all the potters of whom we have any record used Sikyatki and/or Payupki design units on at least one piece of pottery in the collection. Thus all of them can be said to have participated in, if not contributed to, the Sikyatki Revival Style.

SIKYATKI REVIVAL WARES IN THE MELVILLE COLLECTION

Ceramic wares are commonly defined by their surface color and finish. We can discriminate between six wares, each of which is decorated in the Sikyatki Revival Style. The earliest of these is Polacca Polychrome, Style D. The remaining five wares will be referred to as Sikyatki Revival Polychrome, Polished Red Ware, Red and Buff Ware, Red and White Ware and White Ware. All of these wares tend to fall into a chronological sequence (Figure 5), which seems to have been dictated by Anglo pressures. Polacca Polychrome, Style D, for example, was abandoned because the Hopis and Tewas by 1910 wanted cash to buy things, because American buyers rejected crackled slips and because they insisted on "care or attention to detail," as Fewkes put it. The sequence of the other five Sikyatki Revival Style wares reflects the influence of the Museum of Northern Arizona (Chapter 3) and the nature of Hopi-Tewa relations (Chapter 5).

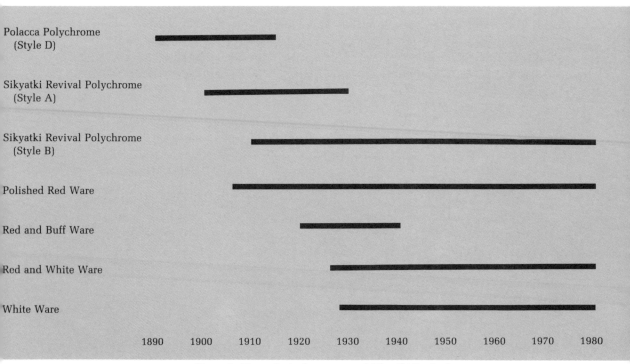

Figure 5. Chronological sequence of Sikyatki Revival wares

Sikyatki Revival Polychrome, like its prehistoric prototype, has a polished, unslipped, or self-slipped, surface which turns buff to yellow-buff on firing. Some examples have yellow-orange fire clouds. The majority of pieces also duplicate Sikyatki Polychrome with regard to paste, which is harder than that used for Polacca Polychrome.

There are two distinguishable types of Sikyatki Revival Polychrome, one of which is known to have developed before the other. It seems reasonable, therefore, to refer to the earlier type as Style A.

In 1903 George Pepper collected a self-slipped vessel made by Nampeyo for the American Museum of Natural History. This vessel (29.0/257), and a number of others that he collected at the same time for the Museum of the American Indian, can be classified as Sikyatki Revival Polychrome, Style A. In this style of Sikyatki Revival Polychrome the black and red colors used for the designs are made with the same pigments used in Polacca Polychrome. They are distinguishable from both prehistoric Sikyatki and other Sikyatki Revival wares because the red and black are more "dense" and the red is "muddy." (This difference in pigments can be seen in the illustration on page 80.) The black and red designs of Sikyatki Revival Polychrome, Style A, were frequently polished, perhaps in order to make them lighter and more like the Sikyatki colors.

There are 10 pieces of Sikyatki Revival Polychrome, Style A in the Melville Collection. Two of these are low bowls, one with and one without a flanged shoulder (Plate 1: center, lower). These low bowls provide a large, relatively flat area for interior decoration (Plate 2). Low bowls have exterior decoration only if they have flanged shoulders. A globular bowl (Plate 1: top) has decoration only on the exterior. The two low bowls and the globular bowl were acquired in 1927 at the Tewa Village.

Two "vases" were also acquired at Hano in 1927 (Plate 3). The red rim on one of these vases and on the globular bowl (Plate 1) is characteristic of Polacca Polychrome. The only two pieces in the collection that are Sikyatki Revival Polychrome, Style A, and for which we do not know either the maker or the village from which they came, are two ladles (Plate 2: upper right; Plate 4: lower left). The ladle in Plate 2 is decorated with dotted crescents and a half scroll with two attached triangles, all of which are associated with Polacca Polychrome. The miniature ladle in Plate 4 was probably made by a child. "Miniatures" have a long history (Smith 1971) and were probably used as children's toys. A child's first attempts at pottery making were often miniatures (Wyckoff n.d. chapter 4:36); but the influx of tourists to the Southwest after 1882 encouraged adult production of miniatures for sale as curios. The four miniatures in Plate 4 are identical in shape to their full size counterparts.

The 10 Sikyatki Revival, Style A pieces in the collection are proof that this variety of pottery persisted until 1927. It is likely, in fact, that it persisted at least until 1930, when it came under attack from the Museum of Northern Arizona. As was mentioned in Chapter 3, the Museum made a survey of Hopi crafts in 1929, after which "steps were taken to check further deterioration" (Colton 1938:19). One of these steps was the establishment, in 1930, of the

Hopi Craftsmen Exhibition and sale, where "inferior pieces were never accepted for exhibition" (Colton 1938:20). The criteria by which vessels were judged included standards for surface finish ("perfectly smooth and glossy") and color. The Museum favored "a consistently good black color" and a red that did "not look splotchy" and was not "a muddy brown instead of red" (Bartlett 1936:3). The Museum was evidently successful in imposing its criteria of excellence on the Hopi and Tewa potters, for the dense, muddy colors of Polacca Polychrome were soon abandoned.

The Museum of Northern Arizona obviously preferred what we are now calling Sikyatki Revival Polychrome, Style B. Remarkable examples of this ware were created by Nampeyo at least as early as 1912, when H. J. Spinden acquired four of her vessels for the American Museum of Natural History (50.1/6688, 6689, 6690, 6691). It is because of the contrast between these vessels and the earlier 1903 vessel, which is also at the American Museum of Natural History, that I question Hough's statement regarding Nampeyo's matching of pigments in 1896. I would surmise that, when he was writing in 1917, he was referring to her later work. In order to clarify the situation, the Nampeyo pieces purchased by him for the Smithsonian should be examined. Tentatively, I would suggest a beginning date of 1910 for Sikyatki Revival Polychrome, Style B.

The technical similarity of Nampeyo's vessels to prehistoric Sikyatki Polychrome is more than enough to account for Fewkes' fears that they would be mistaken for their prehistoric antecedents. The paste, the surface color and lustre, the pigment and the width of line all conform to the earlier prototype. The change from the wider yucca brush used on Polacca Polychrome (approximately .5 cm.) to a narrower yucca brush (approximately .1 cm.) was critical for copying the intricate Sikyatki designs. Nampeyo's brush gradually narrowed until she mastered the line characteristic of the prehistoric ware.

The technological similarity between prehistoric Sikyatki Polychrome and Sikyatki Revival Polychrome, Style B is evident in the 20 Style B pieces in the Melville collection, although only one vessel is Sikyatki in form (page 77). The curios include two ash trays (Plate 12). One is a miniature of the standard dish form and the other is the lady's single cigarette type popular in the early 1900s. There is also a little dish with a coyote figure rising from the rim at the back. Since the coyote figure is perforated, this dish was, presumably, made to be attached to a wall. Boxes or containers with one side higher than the other are still made for sale (Wyckoff n.d. chapter 4:2). There is only one miniature vessel the form of which is clearly derived from prehistoric Sikyatki Polychrome (Plate 12). There is also a ceramic hat and a pair of moccasins (Plate 13). The moccasins are in the shape of the tall, white buckskin, lady's moccasins originally worn in the winter but now reserved for "dress" occasions. The two ceramic moccasins are painted on the exterior, with a different panel on each side. Although both panels utilize Sikyatki design units, one (Plate 13:lower) is reminiscent of the Kachina masks painted on Polacca Polychrome.

These curios demonstrate the creativity of Hopi potters and the variety of

74

objects they produced. The curios probably reflect Anglo taste as much as Hopi humor. It is interesting that, of the four signed Sikyatki Revival Polychrome, Style B pieces, two of them are curios, one being the box with the coyote figure and the other the hat. Stanislawski states that "around 1925–1930 personnel at the Museum of Northern Arizona, and local artists and traders, seem to have encouraged the use of identification marks on Hopi and Hopi-Tewa pottery" (Chapter 3). The earliest mark that he recorded, however, was one made by Sadie Adams in 1930 (Stanislawski, Stanislawski and Hitchcock 1976:51–56). He notes, however, that Hattie Carl (of the Baptist Church), Irene Gilbert, Zella Cheeda, and Paqua Naha were also signing their pieces at this time. The frog painted on the base of the coyote box is an early mark used by Paqua Naha, whose name, "Paqua," means frog. This mark was later used by her descendants (Stanislawski, Stanislawski and Hitchcock 1979: Figure 8).

The base of the hat is marked with a spider. The maker, however, remains unknown. The two pieces signed with a name are a small jar (Plate 14: right) and a bowl (Plate 7). The jar is signed "Sahyah" and was made by Ethel Salyah, sometimes written "Sahyah." The bowl was signed by "Annie Nampeyo," a daughter of Nampeyo.

Red Ware has a red surface, regardless of whether it is slipped. Further research may require different categories for slipped and unslipped vessels; but, unless there are wear marks, slipped and unslipped pieces appear identical, because the slip is made from the same red clay that is used for the unslipped pieces. Moreover, modern potters themselves classify pottery on the basis of surface color, regardless of whether it is slipped. Stanislawski has noted that surface "color styles are recognized by the Hopi-Tewa as being different" (1969:8). Some potters slip a vessel to create a surface color change, rather than shift to a different clay, because they prefer working with one clay rather than another.

Although some prehistoric Red Ware was self-slipped (Smith 1971:422–473), there is no evidence that a red slip was ever used to change the color of a piece until the 1920s. It may be significant that there was a revival of red slipped pottery at Zia Pueblo and at San Ildefonso in the 1920s (Harlow 1977:69, 37).

Undecorated Red and Brown culinary wares (Plate 36) were produced by the Tewas in 1892 (Stephen 1936:102), when the Hopis on First Mesa were making Polacca Polychrome. The two wares were probably exchanged; but, according to Stephen, each of the two ethnic groups specialized in their own pottery type.

There is only one piece of undecorated Red Ware in the Melville Collection (Plate 15), and this was clearly produced for the tourist market. Vessels of this shape and size were commonly used as water canteens, tied to the wearer's belt to carry into the fields for the day. Larger versions were carried with a burden strap on the back. The stopper for the neck was a corncob. The canteen in the Melville Collection, however, is not functional; because, since it has no piñon gum coating, it leaks water. It is made from white clay with a red slip and is signed "Nampaya." This signature is unlike any of the signatures used by potters who are descendants of Nampeyo. If this piece was in fact made by Nampeyo, when her eyes had begun to fail and she no longer painted her work, who signed it for her? Putting an *a* at the end of her name, rather than an *o*, was common Anglo practice until around 1920. This spelling, along with the fact that no pots are known to have been signed, especially prior to firing, by Nampeyo, suggests that an Anglo signed it for her. Such a person would not have been connected with the Museum of Northern Arizona; because the museum staff preferred the spelling "Nampayo."

There are 32 pieces of painted Red Ware in the Melville Collection. Except for two pieces, which are slipped, they are made from red clay. The practice of applying painted decoration to a red vessel was possibly Tewa in origin. If so, this ware could have served as an ethnic marker, a material expression of Tewa ethnicity. The First Mesa Hopis had expressed a proprietary interest in the Polacca Polychrome convention of applying painted designs to a white vessel (Nequatewa 1943). (See also Chapter 5.) Sherds of prehistoric painted red wares, such as Kayenta, Kiet Siel or Jeddito Polychrome, are, however, commonly found in the Hopi area. They are even found at the site of Awatovi (Smith 1971:296–441), adjacent to where Nampeyo collected her clay (Nequatewa 1943:41). Thus, it would seem likely that the introduction of painted Red Ware was a consequence of Tewa ethnicity, American interest in prehistoric wares, and the fact that ancient prototypes were readily available. Although I am not aware of any copies of prehistoric red wares being commissioned by Keam, the fact that he had a variety of prehistoric wares copied, including corrugated and black-on-white wares, would clearly have communicated Anglo interest in prehistoric wares in general, not just Sikyatki Polychrome. I would suggest, therefore, that painted Red Ware was first produced by the Tewas and at a date not long after the appearance of Sikyatki Revival Polychrome.

The earliest recorded piece of painted Red Ware at the Museum of the American Indian (10/50 79) was collected by George Pepper in 1903. This piece, which is shaped like a prehistoric Sikyatki jar (Fig. 4), was collected at the Tewa village. The surface is red and highly polished and is decorated with black and white scrolls. A similar piece, shaped like a prehistoric Sikyatki jar, red and highly polished and decorated in black and white, was made by Nampeyo at about the same time. This vessel (1646) was entered into the collection of the Museum of the American Indian in 1904 or 1905; but of course it may have been made earlier.

Although these jars are both decorated to a greater or lesser degree in the Sikyatki Revival Style, the manner in which white is used is clearly derived from prehistoric Jeddito Polychrome. On the latter, white was used primarily as a narrow outline for the black designs. It was also used occasionally to fill in an area within a black design. It was never used as a designing color.

Two types of painted Red Ware are found in the Melville Collection, which can be distinguished on the basis of surface finish and the use of white. Pol-

SIKYATKI REVIVAL POLYCHROME, Style B
Made by "Lucy's Mother"
Photograph by William K. Sacco

ished Red Ware has a highly polished surface and is probably the same ware as that termed "Sichomovi Polychrome" by Harlow (1977:93). I do not use this term, however, because Harlow states that a red slip is a critical attribute. Polished Red Ware pieces, like the earlier pieces at the Museum of the American Indian, use white only as an outline or, occasionally, as a filler in black designs in the manner of Jeddito Polychrome. There is, therefore, little stylistic difference between vessels decorated solely in black and those which utilize white as well. (See page 80: right.) Again, further research may determine that the use of black, or black and white, are critical distinctions and motivate a subdivision of what I have lumped together as Polished Red Ware. The black pigment used on the Melville Red Ware vessels is the same as that used on Sikyatki Revival Polychrome, Style B vessels.

In the Melville Collection there are twenty-nine pieces of Polished Red Ware (Plates 16–25). The red surface is highly polished and, in two cases, slipped red. One of these slipped pieces is a small tulip vase (Plate 19: center) and the other a bowl (Plate 25: lower).

The tulip vase on the right of Plate 19 is signed "Ethel" and is the only signed Polished Red Ware piece. "Ethel" is the same person who signed her name "Sahyah" on the Sikyatki Revival Polychrome, Style B jar (Plate 14: right) and who wrote the letter quoted in Chapter 2. Salyah, or Sahyah, was Ethel's husband's name, which Ethel took as her surname when white officials required that the Indians use both given names and surnames. They probably encouraged married women to take their husbands' names, an idea totally foreign to the matrilineal Hopis and Tewas (Chapter 5).

Apart from the elongated tulip or cylindrical vases, there are only two vessels which can be considered either jars or vases. These are both decorated solely in black. One was originally made as a lamp base with an accompanying shade decorated with Sikyatki designs (Plate 21). This lamp and shade were probably ordered by Mrs. Melville and, if so, were made after 1927.

There are thirteen Polished Red Ware miniatures and curios. All of the miniatures are made from red clay with the exception of the miniature bowl (Plate 22: center, right), which is slipped red. The seven smaller miniatures (Plate 23: upper and center right; and Plate 22) have been pinched into a variety of shapes. Except for one jar and a bowl, the decoration on the miniatures is entirely black. None of the decorations on these pieces follow Sikyatki design precepts. One piece is decorated with tadpoles, commonly used on ceremonial vessels; another has a centralized swastika form and the jar, which utilizes white as well as black, is decorated with a geometric design derived from Jeddito Polychrome. In contrast to the smaller miniatures, the larger miniatures (Plate 23: center left and lower and Plate 24) are decorated with Sikyatki Revival Style designs.

It is interesting that all of these miniatures vary in form as well as design. The only plaque in the collection (Plate 25: upper) and an effigy head (Plate 24: upper) are Polished Red Ware. Both of these pieces are made from red clay and painted in black and white. The design on the plaque or "hot plate" is of a Polacca Polychrome style bird with a round head topped by a crest and a triangular beak and body. The manufacture of flat ceramic plaques or tiles for sale to tourists was encouraged by Keam in the 1880s, according to Wade and McChesney (1981:455).

The effigy head, although made in the form of a deep globular pot with the addition of pinched lugs, is non-functional as it has a large open mouth. This piece combines Cochiti Pueblo sculpture with a Hopi design. The face itself, with its large open mouth, slit eyes, pierced nostrils and ears, as well as painted sideburns, is very similar to figures which have been manufactured at Cochiti Pueblo since the 1880s (Harlow 1977:55). Across the back of the head, however, is painted an isolated Sikyatki Revival design like that seen on the exterior of bowls in Plates 5 and 32.

In addition to the Polished Red Ware, there are also Unpolished Red Ware pieces with painted designs in the Melville Collection. None of these are decorated with Sikyatki Revival designs and are, therefore, not Sikyatki Revival pieces. They are also distinguished by the fact that white is used as a designing color, not simply to outline or fill black designs. The fact that Sikyatki Revival designs are found only on highly polished pottery evidently results from the fact that the fine lines of Sikyatki Revival Style designs can only be executed on a smooth surface.

The Unpolished Red Ware bowl represented in Plate 26 is of a shape that was common throughout the Polacca Polychrome period, according to Wade and McChesney (1981:560), and is the same shape as the stew bowls that are currently used on Third Mesa. This bowl may have been intended for use as a stew bowl and may well have been made on Third Mesa. Its interior design, which has large figures around a central axis, and also its exterior design, consisting of semi-circles repeated along the rim line, are typical of traditional Third Mesa ceramics (Wyckoff n.d. chapter 4:105). The red clay with brown spots from which the bowl was made is of a type commonly used by Third Mesa potters.

The remaining Unpolished Red Ware pieces are a box (Plate 27) and a doll's house complete with figures and a miniature bowl (Plate 28). Both are made from red clay. The box has house walls, which are painted in black and white on each side, and a female effigy at each end with hair whorls indicating puberty. These are almost identical to effigies collected by Keam in the 1890s (Wade and McChesney 1981:446). The maidens' cloaks fall from their shoulders down the two ends of the box. Because these sections of the box have been painted or slipped white, the box might be classified as Red and White Ware. Ceramic boxes were used as containers for salt (Hough 1918:239) or prayer meal. This box was probably made to contain a child's play things, such as strips of cloth, bone dolls or ceramic miniatures. The doll's house (Plate 28) with its family was also probably made for a child and not for sale. The figurine of the maiden is similar to early Polacca Polychrome figures, which were slipped in white. Hough collected similar materials in 1896 and wrote that "objects in miniature are made for children. The potter constructs toy vessels, rattles and dolls, and sometimes manufactures models of houses" (1918:290).

SIKYATKI REVIVAL WARES
Left: Sikyatki Revival Polychrome, Style A (upper)
Sikyatki Revival Polychrome, Style B (lower)
Right: Polished Red Ware
Photograph by William K. Sacco

It would appear, therefore, that all the Unpolished Red Ware pieces in the collection were manufactured for use and not for sale. Unfortunately, we do not know who made them or in which villages they were acquired. In 1892 Stephen (1936:1021) noted that only the Hopis of First Mesa made figurines, whereas the Tewas did "not understand the art." These pieces may, therefore, have been made by "traditional" Hopis (Chapter 4) who were not manufacturing Sikyatki Revival wares for sale.

Another ware decorated with Sikyatki Revival style designs is what I have termed Red and Buff Ware. This ware was made from white clay, the same as that commonly used for Sikyatki Revival Polychrome vessels, and at least fifty percent of the piece was slipped red. The entire vessel or object was then highly polished.

The four Red and Buff Ware vessels are, visually, quite distinct from Polished Red Ware vessels because the decoration is confined to the sections which have not been slipped red. The only unslipped sections on the two large vessels (Plate 29) form exterior bands. These bands have been painted with Sikyatki Revival designs in black and red. The red areas on the exterior portions of these vessels are reminiscent of some Polacca Polychrome vessels (Wade and McChesney 1981:104). A red base, representing approximately 50% of the exterior surface, is commonly found on Payupki Polychrome; and a red underbody is characteristic of vessels from Zia which were made during the 1920s. Payupki Polychrome may also be the source for the shape of the jar (Plate 29:left).

The two miniature Red and Buff Ware vessels (Plate 30) each have one entire surface which has been slipped red and the other which is left unslipped. This dual division is characteristic of Red and White Ware, in which one surface is slipped white and the other is left red. As these two pieces do not use a white slip I have temporarily classified them as Red and Buff Ware; but further research utilizing a larger sample may necessitate a reclassification of these pieces. For the present, it is important to note that the only slip used on the miniatures is red and that this is only on the exterior. It was during the mid 1920s that Maria and Julian of San Ildefonso began making red exterior—white interior vessels (Harlow 1977:37). The Hopi area potters developed Red and Buff Ware, apparently in the mid 1920s. This ware may have been developed to compete with the Rio Grande tourist ceramic trade and apparently was strictly a tourist ware. It appears that Red and Buff Ware was not produced after about 1940.

What Stanislawski (1969) has referred to as the "red exterior-white interior style" I am simply calling Red and White Ware. It has been proposed that this ware may have been developed in the late 1950s; but this is clearly not the case, as four of these vessels, as well as curios, in the Melville collection were acquired in 1927. Stanislawski (1969) has suggested that this ware may have been developed by potters who had difficulty in firing vessels slipped entirely in white. In contrast to the crackled white slip of Polacca Polychrome, Red and White Ware has a hard, smooth, chalk white slip. According to the potters with whom Stanislawski spoke in 1968, it is extremely difficult to fire the white slip as it will fire cloud "if allowed to touch the fuel, if there are heat flares, or if it is removed from the fire when hot" (Stanislawski 1969). This slip is used only on the interior of Red and White Ware, where it is protected from both fuel and heat flares. Considering that a light, buff interior is characteristic of Red and Buff Ware and that this same dual combination was popular at San Ildefonso, however, I do not believe that technical limitations determined the development of Red and White Ware, which by 1940 had replaced Red and Buff Ware.

There are nine pieces of Red and White Ware in the Melville Collection. Although decorated with Sikyatki and Payupki design units, one jar is also decorated with a Polacca Polychrome style bird (Plate 32). Another (Plate 33: upper) is unusual in both its decoration and form. This jar is decorated on the exterior with Sikyatki Revival designs painted in black between which is a raised, gouged, white slipped, undulating band. This band, which actually consists of two coils, is similar to the snake border on the kilts of the Snake Dancers and of the *Wuyak-kusta* and *Hilili* Kachinas. The shape of this vessel may also have been derived from the Payupki Polychrome jar form (Figure 4). Vessels of this same shape and size are still occasionally made on Third Mesa to contain prayer sticks. This jar, and the curios, are made from the same white clay that is commonly used for Sikyatki Revival Polychrome and for Polished Red Ware as well as Red and Buff Ware.

The curios consist of a "hanging" vessel (Plate 34), a set of four napkin rings (Plate 34), and an effigy vessel in the form of a human head (Plate 33). Although this vessel has black painted sideburns, eyes and a mouth, its features are markedly different from those of the Polished Red Ware effigy (Plate 24). The rounder eyes and slit mouth are similar to earlier Hopi figurines (Wade and McChesney 1981:447) but not to the Cochiti style figure. Moreover, the Red and White effigy has pierced nostrils but not pierced ears.

White Ware is represented by four vessels in the Melville Collection. According to Stanislawski (1969, 1978), White Ware cannot be traced back further than 1927, when it was exhibited at a fair in San Diego. The four vessels represented in Plate 35, therefore, must represent some of the earliest examples of this ware. The chalk white slip on three of these vessels is completely devoid of fire cloud marks. Only the tulip vase is slightly clouded. As Stanislawski has indicated, this ware involves not only the use of a new slip but, because of the difficulty in firing this slip, different firing techniques. Coal, as opposed to dung, has become the preferred fuel for White Ware. The tall jar was made by Sellie, the same potter who made a similar shaped Red and White Ware container (Plate 33). Like the Red and White Ware jar this piece is decorated with a raised undulating "snake band" and Sikyatki design units. This band, however, is red. The tulip shaped vase, cup, and basket are also decorated with Sikyatki designs in black and red on the white slip. Tadpoles, which were occasionally used in prehistoric Sikyatki designs, cross the handles of the basket. These three pieces were evidently made by the same potter.

White Ware and Red and White Ware, as well as the antecedent Red and Buff Ware, were probably developed in response to the American tourists' insatiable demand for something "typical" and, at the same time, "new and different". Not only are these two wares still popular today (page 37), but the demand for White Ware continues to increase. The popularity of this ware may reflect the contemporary American emphasis on clarity of design or the "slick" quality referred to in Chapter 3.

THE SIKYATKI REVIVAL STYLE

The Sikyatki Revival Style, which flourished between approximately 1900 and 1940, is both linear and baroque. The baroque scrolls were primarily continued from Polacca Polychrome. Polacca Polychrome design was derived from the very similar Zuni Polychrome. The painted scrolls and other designs on these vessels (Plate 51) are quite distinct from the background, which is the surface of the vessel. The scroll on the Zuni vessel is commonly referred to as a "Rain Bird" design (Mera 1937). If this scroll is compared to the scrolls on the Sikyatki Revival Polychrome bowl (page 77) it can be seen that, although the scroll is used, this separation between figure and ground is no longer maintained. This is because of two factors: a finer line is used to outline the scroll and, secondly, the designs within the scroll utilize figure-ground reversal. Thus, the designs within the scrolls appear as buff, the color of the background, rather than as black, the color of the painted scroll.

In order to create figure-ground reversal or "negative designs" (Shepard 1956:288–293) the size of the filled area must be greater than, or approximately the same as the ground area (Wyckoff n.d. chapter 4:110). This can be seen in the two pieces at the bottom of Plate 16. Figure-ground reversal can also be created by surrounding the negative figure with a painted area, as seen in the vessel illustrated on page 77.

The repetitious use of figure-ground reversal in the Sikyatki Revival Style is also dependent on geometric forms. Between 1900 and approximately 1940, however, geometric designs remain subservient to flowing, curved lines. It is the emphasis on line that probably appealed so much to contemporary Anglo taste. Barilli (1969:17–18), in his discussion of a contemporary Anglo style, states that "the most obvious stylistic traits of Art Nouveau are fluid forms . . . and . . . . undulating lines. Many Art Nouveau works are composed of a multitude of small, intensely vibrant parts that either complement linear rhythms or in effect constitute a surrogate for them." Although somewhat simpler and, perhaps, with a greater emphasis on the surface plane, this description is also applicable to Art Deco and the pre-1940 Sikyatki Revival style. The latter differs from the previous Polacca Polychrome style in that, within the same design, it combined the geometric, those "small intensely vibrant parts," with an undulating linear style. This dramatic combination was in part created by new design layouts.

The exteriors of most Sikyatki, Payupki and Polacca Polychrome vessels are decorated with framed bands. A framed band is a long strip of decoration encircling the vessel and contained within two framing lines. This band on Sikyatki Polychrome jars was commonly divided into panels and usually encircled the jar at its maximum diameter, which was the shoulder. Occasionally, the upper portion of the jar was painted. Payupki jars were decorated with panelled framed bands on the upper half of the vessel. Polacca Polychrome jars usually had a band about the body and one encircling the neck. Although these bands were occasionally subdivided, the design consisted for the most part of a series of isolated figures within the framing lines. Sikyatki and Payupki bowls were usually not painted on the exterior. When Sikyatki bowls were decorated on the exterior, however, they had two, or four, isolated designs, as seen on the exterior of the Sikyatki Revival Polychrome bowl, page 77. Polacca Polychrome bowls, in contrast to the earlier polychromes, were almost always decorated on the exterior with panelled framed bands.

Although some Sikyatki Revival Style bowls utilize the prehistoric Sikyatki bowl exterior layout (Plates 1, 5 and 32), the framed band continued as the preferred exterior bowl design layout (Plates 1, 4, 6, 7, 17, 24 and 29). Perhaps because of the popularity of bowls as tourist items the framed band has, since approximately 1940, become the dominant design layout for the exterior of both bowls and jars. This layout created a rigid, geometric style in contrast to the curvilinear style which was dominant in the first half of the century. Between approximately 1920 and 1940, the framed band continued in use on bowl exteriors, but was replaced by the "extended band" layout on the exterior of jars and vases. In this layout, the outlines of the scroll are used as the base framing line. The dramatic stylistic difference between these two layouts can be seen by comparing the two vessels illustrated in Plate 3. The inspiration for the extended band exterior design layout may have been the desire to combine the Sikyatki band with the Polacca scroll, or simply the conversion of a Sikyatki bowl interior layout to vase exteriors.

There were six basic Sikyatki interior bowl design layouts. Two of these were asymmetric. In one the design figure occupied a horizontal section of the design field (See Fewkes 1898 Pl. CXXXVIII—c, Pl. CXXIX f). This type of layout was not used by Sikyatki Revival style potters. The other asymmetric layout consisted of a curved form which partially encircled a negative central axis point. This was not a common Sikyatki layout, but was utilized by Sikyatki Revival style potters. As this type of layout (Plate 16: lower) was not used on Polacca Polychrome, it is a dramatic departure from the immediately preceding style. This layout is, however, in the shape of the Polacca Polychrome scroll. In order to create this layout, where the central focal point is background, the background must be conceived as being as important as the painted area. This value placed on the background is also implicit in figure-ground reversal, when the background must be conceived as a potential design.

Polacca interior bowl designs almost always had positive central axis points. This type of layout is seen in the Polished Red Ware plaque (Plate 25:

upper) and miniature (Plate 23: middle right). Prehistoric Sikyatki Poly-chrome bowl interiors also utilized symmetric, positive, central axis layouts, but also symmetric, negative, central axis layouts, as in Plate 16 (upper left). In this example the negative central circle is surrounded by split feather designs of the sort found commonly on Payupki and occasionally on Polacca Polychrome.

Two more Sikyatki bowl interior layouts were the horizontal band and the extended band. The horizontal band consisted of a band which crossed the bowl interior. The extended band was not as widely used as the horizontal band, but later became the preferred bowl interior layout of Sikyatki Revival potters. This type of layout can be seen on vessels illustrated in Plate 2: lower left, Plate 5, Plate 16: upper right and center, and Plate 23: lower left. The extended band was one of the layouts used to create the one third to two thirds spatial division, an attribute of many prehistoric Sikyatki interior designs. The division of the interior area of a bowl into two design sections, one being approximately twice the size of the other, was a radical departure from the earlier Polacca bowl interior layouts. This type of spatial division was probably not used by Sikyatki Revival potters until sometime between 1910 and 1915. One of Nampeyo's Sikyatki Revival Polychrome pieces at the American Museum of Natural History, which were collected by H. J. Spinden in 1912, used this type of division (50.1/6691). It is not, however, decorated with the extended band layout but rather with an upper band and, in the larger section, a scroll. None of the earlier Sikyatki Revival Polychrome, Style A pieces at the Museum of the American Indian utilize either this type of division or the extended band. Thus, I would surmise that this type of division was not used until approximately 1910, and that it only became popular with the use of the extended band layout, which was not extensively used until around 1920. By 1924, however, this type of layout had become the preferred type (Bunzel 1929: Appendix II). As this type of layout did not become popular until the 1920s it is not commonly associated with Sikyatki Polychrome, Style A and does not occur on any of these vessels in the Melville Collection. The two Sikyatki Revival Polychrome, Style A bowls and the ladle which are decorated on the interior are illustrated in Plate 2 (upper, and lower right). The design on the ladle is almost identical to that found on Polacca Poly-chrome ladles (see Wade and McChesney 1981: Pl. IV: 23–26). Although in essence a Polacca design, utilizing such Polacca design units as the semi-circle filled with dots, the descending double triangle or "split feather", and scroll tip with appended triangles, the upper section has been enlarged to contain the two dotted semi-circles. The extent to which this area is filled in with black paint, together with the thickness of line, makes the upper section so heavy that the one third/two thirds division is not apparent. This is also the situation with the adjacent bowl (upper left). On this vessel, triangles extend towards the middle from the upper one third section, and also towards the middle from the base line. The result is a negative center; but the layout does not adhere to prehistoric Sikyatki design precepts. The third Sikyatki Revival, Style A interior design represented in Plate 2 (bottom right) consists of a central band in the prehistoric Sikyatki style, but to this design has been added "buds" very similar to the Polacca Polychrome three point split feather (Wade and McChesney 1981:584). This layout, like that of the ladle, utilizes a positive central axis.

If the decoration on the three Sikyatki Revival Style A pieces illustrated in Plate 2 are compared with the Style B vessel on the lower left the stylistic difference between these layouts and the fully developed extended band layout can easily be seen. The extended band (Plate 2: lower left) is a finely drawn scroll. This type of layout is linear. In 1924 Nampeyo stated that: "For the bowl I always use a one line design. It must start from the 'road line' and come back into it again" (Bunzel 1929:42). Certainly Nampeyo was a master of the use of line, but she was not alone. According to Bunzel (1929:42), First Mesa potters were all acutely aware of the importance of line. It is the extended band layout, which utilizes the geometric band in conjunction with a curvilinear extension, or an adaptation of this layout, that was used on the exterior of vases and tall jars.

The question can be asked as to whether this layout was used on bowl interiors prior to the introduction of the tulip vase form, or whether, in seeking an appropriate layout for this new form, the potters turned to known Sikyatki layouts and began simultaneously to use the extended band layout on both bowl interiors and vase exteriors. If this layout was not used prior to the introduction of the tulip vase form, then indeed Anglo taste, albeit indirectly, did influence the Sikyatki style itself. Unfortunately, the question cannot be answered until we reconstruct the chronology of the relevant shapes and designs. Tentatively, it would seem to me more likely that the extended band layout was first used on the interior of bowls and then adapted to the vase form. However, this layout was already preferred for the exterior of the tulip vase by 1924 (Bunzel 1929:42).

The Melville Collection provides a unique opportunity for the study of the relationship between layout and vessel form. As we know many of the individual makers, we also know that all the potters produced a variety of vessel forms and utilized different layouts appropriate to the form as well as size of a given vessel. The six vessels made by Ethel Salyah provide an excellent example. Her small (height 8.4 cm., diameter at rim 10.8 cm.) bowl (Plate 10: left) is decorated with a panelled band. A larger (height 13.0 cm., diameter at rim 15.9 cm.) deep bowl or low jar (Plate 20) is decorated with a panelled band to which feathers have been attached horizontally and "arrows" have been attached vertically. This is a modified extended band layout. The extended band layout was used on her taller, narrower jar (height 15.4 cm., diameter at rim 11.2 cm.). The two tulip vases (Plate 19: right and left) are also decorated with extended bands. On these vessels, however, the horizontal band is negligible in comparison to the extended area, which also forms a panelled band. Thus, the primary band shifts from horizontal to vertical as the ratio of height to rim diameter increases.

Ethel was not unique in her adaptation of designs to vessel shape. Sellie decorated her single bowl (Plate 29: left) with a framed panelled band and her two vases with extended framed bands. Ruth Takala also produced a variety of vessel forms. She preferred isolated unit designs, but on tulip vases (Plate 18: left) these were always horseshoe shaped bands, which are unique to the Sikyatki Revival style. The flowing line, as well as specific units within the design, may come from Sikyatki Polychrome but, like the other potters, she selectively adapted elements of Sikyatki, Payupki, and Polacca Polychrome to create a new and vital style.

As this radical new style shows little or no continuity with the preceding Polacca Polychrome, it has been interpreted as merely commercial, and devoid of cultural content. Bunzel reasoned that it was probably because the potters "assimilated a fully developed artistic style" (1929:71) that "designs, when they have any significance at all, are pictures of material objects" (1929: 70). I would argue, however, that the early Sikyatki Revival potters selectively chose the majority of designs from prehistoric Sikyatki and Payupki Polychromes as they continued Polacca iconography. Thus, in spite of stylistic change, continuity is to be found in the meaning of the designs themselves.

All designs are composed of elements, such as lines and dots, which can be arranged in formalized design units. Some elements, like circles and triangles are more complex and may differ stylistically. Sikyatki Revival potters adapted some elements from Sikyatki Polychrome (Figure 3: lower right). Certain Sikyatki and Payupki design units utilized by Sikyatki Revival potters (Figure 3: lower left) were probably adopted solely for decorative reasons. Others may have been meaningful motifs when they were first incorporated into the design of Sikyatki Revival Polychrome.

Figure 3 (page 68) illustrates design units derived from prehistoric Sikyatki and Payupki Polychrome. The top row consists of three- and two-stepped pyramids. Today, as in the 1900s, this figure is found on Kachina costumes (Plates 42–44) and is the shape of the sides of ceremonial vessels (Stephen 1936:845). It is always identified as a rain cloud. Stephen also identified this figure painted on kiva walls in the 1890s (Stephen 1936:237), as well as on Polacca Polychrome (Wade and McChesney 1980:31). This same figure can be seen on the Zuni vessel, coeval with Polacca Polychrome, illustrated in Plate 51 (lower). This figure surely represents a rain cloud, although it is painted in the Zuni style.

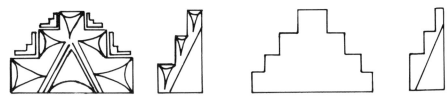

Rain cloud motif from Polacca Polychrome   *Rain cloud motif from Sikyatki Revival Polychrome*

The design units in the second row of Figure 3 are today always identified as feathers, usually as "prayer feathers" (Wyckoff n.d. chapter 4:61–63). I think there can be little doubt that, when copied from Sikyatki and Payupki Polychrome, these design units were recognized as feathers, since these forms, as seen on the far right, represented the wings and tails of birds painted on kiva walls (Stephen 1936:1025) and also prayer feathers in altar paintings dating from the 1890s (Stephen 1936:563, 1025). With the adoption of these design units there was no longer a need for the Polacca bird represented in Plates 25 and 32, one mode of representing a bird or feather having replaced the other.

None of the remaining prehistoric Sikyatki or Payupki design units are referred to by name by modern potters. It may be, however, that this was not the situation in the early 1900s. The designs in the third row are stylistically related to the rain clouds as painted on the scraper for the rasp in Plate 40. This rendition of rain clouds was commonly used in the 1890s (Stephen 1936) and is used today on *Kachina* costumes, Butterfly Dancers' robes, and ceremonial vessels (Wyckoff n.d. chapter 4:63). It is always identified as a rain cloud or rain clouds. That the design units in row three were important symbols which have now lost their original meaning, is indicated by the fact that at the time they were painted on Sikyatki Polychrome, they were also extensively painted on kiva walls (Smith 1952) and occasionally on Polacca Polychrome (Wade and McChesney 1981:299–300, 423). This implies that they remained meaningful until sometime after 1900.

This was probably the case for the first two designs in the fourth row. The crook was, according to Stephen, labeled as representing either a hunting weapon or *mu-ing-wa* (procreative power of life):

> It also appears as a decoration on [Polacca] pottery in this Ꙅ, form and although retaining its name, it is said to signify a root. Again it appears as a scroll-like curve ᎤᎧ. . . . (Stephen, as quoted in Wade and McChesney 1981:31).

Thus Stephen made it clear that the scroll figures on Polacca Polychrome are the same as the angular forms found on rock etchings. The Sikyatki Revival potters may have recognized the Sikyatki crook as a geometric version of the Polacca scroll. If so the Revival potters merely changed from a curved to an angular form.

The two design units on the right of the fourth row may simply have been copied as decorative design units from Sikyatki Polychrome. They are, however, so similar to dragon flies that I would guess this to be their meaning. Dragon flies are frequently found associated with tadpoles and butterflies. Tadpoles were painted on Sikyatki Polychrome vessels as well as Polacca Polychrome ceremonial vessels (Stephen 1936:743). They are still used on ceremonial vessels. Butterflies, like dragon flies, were not painted on Polacca Polychrome ceremonial vessels. They were, however, painted on ceremonial tiles (Stephen 1936:617). Thus, tadpoles and butterflies were painted by Polacca potters, but only on ceremonial objects. Sikyatki Revival potters placed these motifs on commercial pieces. In this respect it is interesting to note that the two butterflies on Melville vases (Plates 3 and 10) use what today is known as the "Four Corner" motif as heads. This motif is referred to in Hopi as *hoysicvi* (*hoy* 'move', *sicvi?o*—'crosswise, roundabout') and symbolizes the Hopi lands and the migrations to it. It has been described by Hopis as:

the sacred circle, it is the land given to us, when we first arrived, by Masau. We came from the four corners [directions] to this land. We all met in the Middle [where the lines intersect]. Our land is sacred and these [the four circles] are the four sacred mountains [these four mountains are Laloma Point–east, San Francisco Peaks–west, Navajo Mountain–north and Woodruff Butte–south] (Wyckoff n.d. chapter 4:65).

Since land is a divine gift, as is life itself, this design unit is, like all the other motifs, associated with the ethereal world and its gifts.

As Bunzel hypothesized (1929:70), motifs do represent "material objects;" but associated with these material objects are religious beliefs and the ceremonial cycle. Why then has it been commonly argued (Bunzel 1929, Douglas 1934, Hubert 1937, Sikorski 1968) that Sikyatki Revival designs are in no way symbolic? I believe there are two reasons for this: firstly, the writers' definition of symbolic and, secondly, the fact that many of the design units have lost their meaning since 1900.

Hubert (1937:1) adheres to Douglas' definition of symbol as "the representation of abstract ideas or qualities by signs arbitrarily selected." By this definition Hopi motifs are not symbolic; they are seen as drawings of the subject itself. As illustrations, the referent is commonly agreed upon but the abstract associations will vary. Today, for example, all Hopis will identify a tadpole as such, although one informant may emphasize how they appear in rock pools if the Kachinas have brought the spring rains whereas another will emphasize that without rain there cannot be life. I would surmise that it was partly because of these varying associations, as well as the fact that some design units are not named motifs, that Bunzel concluded that Sikyatki Revival designs were not symbolic, for "this same element may be differently designated in different contexts" (1929:69). Sikorski, like Bunzel, recognizes that some design units are called rain clouds and feathers, for example, but goes on to state that

"these have no more significance than the names we have given to embroidery stitches. The cross stitch has no connotations of theology, nor do we embroider sacred symbols on doilies. There is no more reason to believe Hopi potters would cover their commercial wares with weighty symbols" (1968:20).

In the light of this statement, it seems that an important problem remains unresolved. Did the potters who presented their works to Sikorski for the Museum of Northern Arizona's 1959 Hopi Show consider these motifs significant and, if not, why not?

In conclusion, the Sikyatki Revival Style is, stylistically, in sharp contrast to the preceding Polacca Polychrome style. This new style incorporated and adapted Sikyatki and Polacca vessel forms as well as layouts; but the reintegration of old and new elements led inevitably to the creation of new vessel forms and new layouts. The Sikyatki Revival emphasized the line of Sikyatki Polychrome, as well as many Sikyatki and Payupki design units; and, although the potters abandoned most Polacca design units, they did not abandon Polacca iconography. This is not to say, however, that some Sikyatki Revival motifs which initially expressed a continuity of the basic cultural belief system may not have gradually lost their meaning. Some understanding of the antecedents of Sikyatki Revival pottery and the context in which it developed can surely provide insights into the direction and momentum of cultural change on the Hopi Mesas during the first half of the twentieth century.

THE POTTERS AND THE AMERICAN ROAD

On the base of one vessel Mrs. Melville wrote in pencil "Maxie." We do not know who Maxie was. On the base of another vessel the smudged pencil marks appear to read "Amay Telatva." A third potter marked her vessel with a spider. None of these potters are remembered today by the members of the First Mesa Baptist Church at Polacca, although all three may have been members in 1927. The Melvilles probably bought their pottery either through potters associated with the Baptists or from the trader, Tom Pavatea. Apart from the two pieces mentioned above, we know that all the pieces on the bottom of which the name of the maker is written in pencil were made by members, or, in one case, the mother of a member, of the Baptist church. Lucy, whose mother was the potter, Ruth, Ethel and Sellie were Baptists.

Ruth Takala was the daughter of Judge Hooker (Hongavi) and Sehepmana, some of the first people from First Mesa to be baptized in the Baptist church. Thus, Ruth spent all or most of her life in a culturally ambivalent position. The tragedy of the time, and it is still often the case, is that Anglos viewed these people as "primitive" and "deprived." Some attempted to take on Anglo ways, to follow the American Road, but were met with Anglo prejudice. Early members of the Baptist church were caught between Hopi, Tewa and Anglo pressures. As one church member told Florence Means (1960:84), "we are so few, and all around us on the mesas are those who do not believe; and they laugh at us." Most of Hongavi's and Sehepmana's children did not remain Baptists; Ruth did probably because her husband, Takala, became a deacon. Ruth was, therefore, like her father, an important member of the group of Christian Indians (illustration on page 41).

Ethel, the wife of Wilfred Salyah, was Tewa. Wilfred had had tuberculosis for many years by 1927. He may have contracted the disease in boarding school. Although the Keams Canyon hospital was already established by 1927, there were no facilities for long term care. Thus, Wilfred lived with his family. The result was that, of their eleven children, only one survived. The Hopis attribute infant mortality to witchcraft on the part of either the mother's or the father's kin. The death of Ethel's and Wilfred's children, therefore, may have served to create suspicion within the extended family. Wilfred's condition, which would have affected his ability to work in the fields, could not be cured, either by traditional medicine men or western doctors. Ethel, like Ruth, was caught between two worlds and chose the Baptist church in her struggle to survive. The church aided her with her sick family, provided her with materials with which to make quilts, and assisted her in

90

the sale of her pottery. Wilfred, who never joined the church, also made articles for sale. He was the maker of the drum and possibly the flute and drill in the Melville collection.

Unfortunately, there is little available information on Lucy and Sellie. Lucy and her mother were Tewas, whereas Sellie was a Hopi. Lucy was, apparently, only marginally involved in the church and her mother was never converted. According to Mrs. Melville, however, Sellie led an "Indian prayer meeting." This meeting was "all in Hopi but most impressive and earnest. About eight were there."

The Melvilles had undoubtedly heard of Nampeyo by the time they arrived at First Mesa. Mrs. Arnold, their daughter, remembers meeting her and her family. The piece by Annie Nampeyo and also the canteen may have been bought directly from Nampeyo's family at this time. Paqua and Lucy's mother were also living in Hano when the Melvilles were there.

Tom Pavatea had established at Polacca what may have been the first Indian owned and operated trading post in the United States. He, like the Nampeyos, Paqua, and Lucy's mother, was a Tewa and not a Baptist. In many ways he befriended the Baptist missionaries, letting them vacation at his sheep camp (Means 1960:88), giving them fruit and candy to be given as Christmas gifts, and providing transportation. In return he was "highly esteemed" by the missionaries "in spite of his refusal of the Way" (Means 1960: 85). The Anglo sculptor, Emory Kopta, was also his friend and rented one of his houses as a studio. Most of the pieces in the Melville collection which are marked in ink as coming from his store are also marked as having been made in the Tewa village of Hano. Thus, the Melville collection consists of pieces made either by Baptists who, except for Ethel, were Hopis, or by Tewas who followed their traditional religion.

In contrast to the Hopis, the Tewas had learned to compartmentalize their social lives. They are consistently referred to by Americans as "friendly" and "progressive." The Tewas' openness to American conveniences and concepts, however, cannot be interpreted as a willingness to assimilate—a point which has been argued at length in Chapter 5. Hopis and Americans are kept at a distance because of their lack of knowledge of the Tewa language and kiva ceremonies. Neither Americans nor Hopis are allowed to enter Tewa kivas. It is this secrecy that permits the Tewas to enter American society and selectively choose that which is advantageous to them without disrupting their ethnic identity. Clearly the Tewas wanted what Americans consider a "high" standard of living. For this reason, no doubt, Tewas accepted wage labor at Keams Canyon, Tom Pavatea opened his trading post, and Nampeyo experimented with pottery for profit. In so doing she accepted assistance from H. R. Voth, the Mennonite missionary; but she did not become a Mennonite, anymore than Tom Pavatea became a Baptist. He and probably most of the Tewa potters befriended the Baptists and used whatever material advantages they had to offer, but never actually joined the church. Ethel Salyah was an exception.

The Hopis had never been defeated, enslaved, or forced to leave their homeland by hostile aliens. They had always managed to avoid the difficulties of dealing with foreigners directly. In such matters they were happy to defer to the Tewas' expertise in dealing with Americans, frequently using Tewas as "go-betweens." When they could not avoid direct contact with Americans the Hopis seem to have responded either by rejecting American goods and concepts (the "Hostile" strategy) or by abandoning most of Hopi tradition and becoming "Friendlies." The divisive effect of American culture and missionization can be seen in village division as at Oraibi.

Hopis, alienated from their traditional culture and frequently from their families, joined others in forming new communities. In the early 1880s the American government had pressed for the relocation of both Hopis and Tewas below their mesa top villages (Nequatewa 1936:131, note 47). Tom Polacca, Nampeyo's brother, was the first person to build in the valley below. It was in his house that the Baptist missionaries first stayed. Polacca's willingness to provide the Baptists with land brought about severe criticism from the Tewas. Gradually, however, many Hopis on First Mesa who were considered "friendly" followed their Tewa neighbors to Polacca. By 1927 most of these Hopis had not only accepted American conveniences, but also Christianity.

Only further research can determine to what extent traditional Tewas and Christian Hopis were responsible for First Mesa ceramic production during the 1920s. These two groups together, however, were certainly the primary producers of Sikyatki Revival wares. If one considers the dynamics of these two groups, it is not surprising that, since 1900, some motifs have lost their original meaning and that American researchers have, upon occasion, been told that other motifs have no meaning whatever. Thus, the design units illustrated in the third row of Figure 3 are no longer called rain clouds as they were in the last century. In this case a specific form of a motif is no longer recognized but another form is. This is apparently not the case with the motif known by Stephen as the mu-ing-wa, the procreative power of life. This is the only named motif which represented a religious abstraction per se, rather than a visible or tangible place or object which had religious associations. It may be that, as the demand for Sikyatki Revival pottery increased and inquiries as to the "meaning" of designs proliferated, traditional Tewa potters ceased to represent the mu-ing-wa in this form. For such potters this motif was, perhaps, more properly considered part of the secret domain, whereas the other motifs could be referred to without providing the information necessary to make a religious association. Thus, these motifs could become part of the "public domain" without violating the integrity of the religion. On pottery, these designs became, to a large extent, commercial decoration lacking a significance given to these same designs in other contexts. This same phenomenon can be observed in the production of Kachina dolls. At first some facet of the Kachina's costume was altered or omitted when the Kachina was portrayed in the form of a doll produced for sale (Dockstader 1954). This is no longer considered necessary however; the doll produced for sale is considered a commercial product and the details of its costume are not perceived as having ritual significance.

92

Although the initial commercialization of Sikyatki Revival pottery was made by traditional Tewas, Americans soon labeled this pottery "Hopi." In the 1920s, as is still the case, other decorative styles were produced (Plate 26), but these ceramics were apparently not in demand and soon were not even considered by the general public to be "Hopi." Hopis wishing to enter into the commercial pottery market were obliged to produce Sikyatki Revival wares. For Baptist Hopis, the use of designs with religious significance must have posed something of a dilemma, for these potters were acutely aware of the significance of such motifs. The degree of Hopi sensitivity to motifs can be seen in the yucca sifters in the Melville collection. The triangular form representing *Co-tuk-i-nung-wa*, the sky god (Wade and McChesney 1980:103) is, through the common yucca weaving process, found in the center of sifters or baskets. In the center of one of the Melville sifters, however, a cross has been woven (Plate 39: lower left). Yucca sifters were not commonly produced for sale; but there was a demand for Sikyatki Revival ceramics. In order to gain a cash income, which would have been in accordance with the missionaries' wishes, these potters painted Sikyatki style motifs. This is perhaps why Hongavi produced the figure in Plate 46, a maiden holding *Mamzrau* Society altar plaques (Stephen 1936:864–973). This was an important woman's ceremony, in many ways the female counterpart of *Wuwuchim*. This figure would never have been made if Salako, its woman chief, and Hongavi had not both joined the Baptist church. With the conversion of Salako, who was baptized shortly after Hongavi, this Hopi society ceased to exist on First Mesa. Like Hongavi, Hopi Baptist potters could use these motifs, acknowledging the objects they represented but disclaiming their religious associations. For these potters, designs representing rain clouds, tadpoles and feathers were labeled but these labels meant nothing more than the name of an embroidery stitch.

Thus, this Sikyatki Revival Style can be considered a commercial style, but it is much more. It has reflected the changes and the continuities of both the Hopi and Tewa societies over the last 80 years. Sikyatki Revival wares have also served as links between Anglos and both Hopi and Tewa societies. Pottery has been bought and sold, and ideas and values have been exchanged, as well as money.

CATALOGUE

HOPIS

Hair brush made from
grass (length 45 cm.)

Approximately two thirds of the Melville collection consists of material collected on the Hopi Reservation in 1927. The ceramics are discussed at length in Chapter 6. The Melvilles, however, were interested in all aspects of Hopi life. They kept *piki* bread, *piñon* nuts, dried corn and strands of dried fiber, all of which are part of the Melville Collection but have not been included in this catalogue. The Melvilles also acquired a *pa·ho*, or "Sun prayer stick" (Stephen 1936:65), which, in deference to Hopi custom and belief, has also been omitted.

The plaques and baskets were acquired either on Second Mesa or from Mr. Womack, who had a garage and store below Second Mesa. The three types of Hopi baskets, coiled yucca, woven rabbit-brush, and plaited yucca, are all represented in the collection. The plaques illustrated in Plate 37 are, except for the plaque at upper right, of the coil type, which is made by coiling and sewing yucca around a foundation of grass or shredded yucca. This type of plaque has been made uniquely on Second Mesa since at least 1930 (Colton 1938:15). Originally only plaques and low walled prayer feather baskets were made by this technique. Probably at the suggestion of traders, deep baskets (Plate 38: left and front) were introduced for the Anglo market. It was either the large deep basket on the left or the even larger woven rabbit-brush basket at the top of Plate 38, that Mrs. Melville, according to her diary, purchased from Omawu on Second Mesa for $5.00. Omawu, like many of the potters from whom the Melvilles made purchases, was a Baptist (Means 1960:109).

The woven rabbit-brush baskets and plaques were more commonly made on Third Mesa. Like the coiled yucca baskets, they were originally limited to plaques (Plate 37: upper right) and low walled ceremonial baskets (Colton 1938:16). Large utilitarian baskets had been made with both warp and weft composed of wild currant. These continued to be made; but rabbit-brush replaced currant for the weft in the large baskets made for the tourist market, since rabbit-brush can be dyed (Plate 38: top and right; Plate 39: lower right).

The third type of basketry is the utilitarian, plaited yucca basket, which is still commonly made on all three mesas (Plate 39).

In the Melville Hopi collection there are musical instruments: a large painted ceremonial drum, a rasp and resonator, and gourd rattles with cottonwood handles (Plate 40). Originally the rattles had prayer feathers attached to the tips. These were used by the Kachinas, who danced to their beat as well as to the drum.

The rasp is commonly played by the *Hemis Mana* at the *Niman* or Home Dance. The Hopi rasp with resonator has a distinctive sound. The resonator in the Melville collection is a gourd painted to look like a dotted turtle. The turtle is associated with water and the dots probably represent rain. The rasp is placed across the top of this gourd resonator and rubbed with the scapula.

The flute in the Melville collection, which is without a plug, was probably made for sale. It is atypical in that is has a decorative "bell" and six rather than five holes. (See Hough 1918:1651.)

The two artifacts in the center of Plate 41 are, from left to right, a spindle with a wooden weight and a pump drill. The pump drill was never used and, like the flute, may well have been made specifically for the Melvilles. This drill would have had a chert or other "flint" point. The horizontal bar was moved up and down to rotate the vertical axis (Bloom 1936:117). This instrument was used until around 1900 (Hough 1918:276).

The object on the far right of Plate 41 is referred to as a boomerang or rabbit stick. This latter term is more accurate as it does not return to the thrower. Simple clubs were thrown to kill a variety of small game; but this type of club or stick was specifically intended for the communal rabbit hunt. It has sections painted red and a black design representing rabbits' feet (Hough 1918: 287).

The bow and arrow on the left is not a weapon but a gift of the Kachina. Small bows and arrows, and occasionally rattles, are given to uninitiated boys at *Powamu*, also known as the Bean Dance. According to some Hopis, these gifts are intended to remind the boys that "they are to protect the Hopi in this world and the next." Girls are given kachina dolls. Like the bow and arrow, these dolls are not given as "toys," in the American sense of the word, but rather as religious educational devices. They can be equated with paintings of the life of Christ that hang in a parochial school classroom. In the early literature (Bourke 1884:264) they were sometimes incorrectly referred to as "idols." Dockstader (1954:97-101) has attributed these figures to the inspiration of Spanish *santos*. It may be, however, that the Hopis adopted their kachina dolls from the Zunis, who may well have taken the idea from the early Spanish church. The earliest known kachina dolls were collected in 1852 (Dockstader 1954:101) and were all associated with the Zuni *Shalako* ceremony. The central doll in Plate 42 is a *Polik Mana* and, like most of the earlier dolls, is flat. The Melville piece has carved lower arms, whereas the arms on earlier pieces were only painted. The technique of painting in, rather than carving, the arms is seen on the *Oöqöle Kachina* (Plate 42: upper left). The adjacent figure is of the same Kachina, but with carved arms and legs. The cylindrical *Oöqöle* and the *Polik Mana* probably date from between 1900 and 1920 and were repainted, as is commonly done, at the time of the Melvilles' visit. The lower kachina in Plate 42, seen from both the front and the side, is an *Ai* or Rattle Kachina. Its mask is like the rattles used by kachina dancers. The front band depicts the milky way; and the design on either side is sometimes referred to as the moon. Stephen refers to this type of Maltese Cross as the *Mana* or Virgin sign (Wade and McChesney 1980:96). The *Ai* Kachina appears, like *Oöqöle*, on First Mesa at the mixed kachina dances.

The Kachina cult is widespread among the pueblos of the Southwest. If a particular kachina is found to be helpful to the people of one pueblo it may be adopted by those of another. The Hopis adopted the Zuni *Shalako* ceremony and, with it, such kachinas as *Polik Mana* and *Hakto* (Plate 43, lower left and center). At Zuni, *Hakto* is known as *Yamuhakto*. The Hopis also have *Koyemsi* or Mud-head Kachinas (Plate 44: lower row, far left). These are clowns who almost invariably appear with other kachinas. As there is no particular honor associated with the men who function as *Koyemsi* amongst the Hopis, in contrast to the Zunis, it would seem likely that this kachina was also adopted from the Zunis, who refer to it by a similar name, *Koyemshi*.

The *Kahaila* and *Hochani Kachinas* were most assuredly introduced from Keres pueblos on the Rio Grande. *Kohaila* (Plate 43, upper center and right) is a Keresan name and *Hochani* (Plate 43: upper left) is the Keresan word for chief (Wright 1973:120, 185).

The two identifiable kachinas represented in this collection which cannot be derived from non-Hopi antecedents are *Kuwan,* or the colorful *Heheya* Kachina (Plate 43: lower right), and *Umtoinaqa,* or the Shooting Thunder Kachina (Plate 44: lower center and right). The *Heheya* Kachina often dances the *Niman* or Home Dance on First Mesa. The *Umtoinaqa* commonly appears in the mixed dances, but may also act as a guard during the Bean Dance. It is possible that the double, red, warrior bandolier is of Spanish origin. Kachina costumes have changed considerably over time; but not the masks, since the power of the kachina is in the mask.

Kachina dolls are given so that the children may learn to identify and know the ways of each kachina. They may also be used as "dolls." The kachina in the baby's cradle in Plate 45 is also depicted in Plate 44 (upper center). It is, therefore, in a sense a "plaything;" but it teaches the child that the Kachinas are to be loved and tended so that they, in turn, will send their blessings.

The stuffed doll was only introduced after 1890 with the coming of schools and missionaries. Hopi children had, prior to this time, used "bone dolls" (Carlson 1964:5). They must have been surprised by dolls that so explicitly represented Hopi girls and women (Plate 45: upper).

A Hopi woman's dress, sash, shoulder blanket, black stockings, moccasins, a bride's "suit case" and beads were also collected by the Melvilles (Plate 47). The dress, sash and shoulder blanket (Plate 48) were all woven on looms of different sizes. The dress and shoulder blanket are of wool. The sash is made from cotton. Shoulder blankets, which were once an unmarried girl's prized possession, are no longer made, having been replaced by Spanish style shawls. The Hopi dress in this collection is typical of women's dresses after 1900 in that embroidery, buttons and a crochet hem have been added to the basic black dress. The silver buttons appear to be of Navajo manufacture.

Today, as in the 1920s, almost all weaving is done by men, either in their houses or in the kivas. Apparently this was not always the case, as Bourke (1884:134) states that in the 1880s women did most of the weaving, whereas only the men knitted the black stockings (Plate 47). By 1900 the women were weaving dress sashes and the men blankets and blanket dresses (Hough 1918: 248). According to Colton, writing in the 1930s, however, "Among the Hopi, the men are the weavers, while among the Navajo, the women are the weavers" (1938:11). It may be that prior to contact Hopi men wove only ceremonial garments and that weaving only became a male industry under acculturative pressure, first from the Spaniards and then the Americans.

What is commonly called the bride's suitcase is actually a long reed mat. The magnificent white bride's mantel and other personal belongings are placed on top of the mat and rolled up in it so that it does, in fact, act as a suitcase. The bride carries this "suitcase" (or bundle) back to her house after her wedding stay with her new husband's mother.

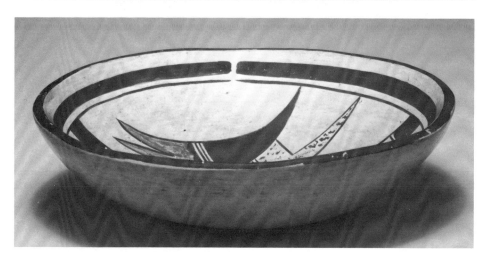

Plate 1. Sikyatki Revival Polychrome, Style A, bowls (Top vessel height: 4.5 cm., interior of middle and lower vessels illustrated in Plate 2)

Plate 2.   Sikyatki Revival Polychrome (Top row and lower right Style A, lower left Style B, diameter at rim 13.7 cm.)

Plate 3.   Sikyatki Revival Polychrome, Style A, vases (Left tulip vase height: 18.9 cm.)

Plate 4. Sikyatki Revival Polychrome, Style A, miniatures (Top vessel height: 10.0 cm.)

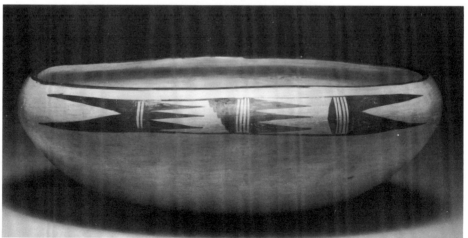

Plate 5. Sikyatki Revival Polychrome, Style B, bowl (Height: 10.3 cm., made by "Lucy's mother")

104

Plate 6.   *Sikyatki Revival Polychrome, Style B, bowl (Height: 6.7 cm.)*

Plate 7. Sikyatki Revival Polychrome, Style B, bowl (Height: 6.6 cm., signed "Annie Nampeyo")

Plate 8.   Sikyatki Revival Polychrome, Style B, jar (Height: 15.4 cm., made by Ethel Salyah)

Plate 9. Sikyatki Revival Polychrome, Style B, jar (Height: 16.3 cm.)

Plate 10. Sikyatki Revival Polychrome, Style B (Left vessel made by Ethel Salyah, upper right vessel made by Amay Telatva [?], lower right vessel height: 6.5 cm.)

109

Plate 11. Sikyatki Revival Polychrome, Style B, bowls (Lower bowl diameter at rim: 9.8 cm.)

Plate 12. Sikyatki Revival Polychrome, Style B, curios (Makers' marks on hat and coyote box also illustrated in Plate 14, top piece height: 8.5 cm.)

Plate 13.   Sikyatki Revival Polychrome, Style B (Height: 10.0 cm.)

Plate 14. Sikyatki Revival Polychrome, Style B (Top vessel height: 10.8 cm., made by Ethel Sal-yah and signed "Sahyah")

113

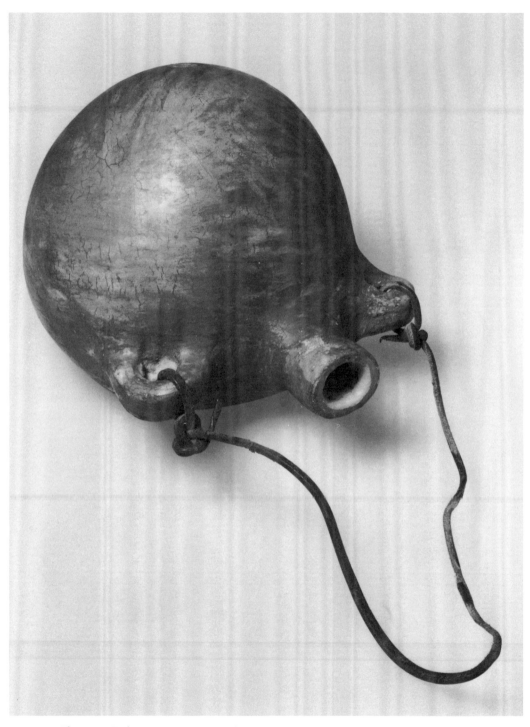

Plate 15.   Red Ware, canteen (Length: 18.2 cm., signed "Nampaya")

114

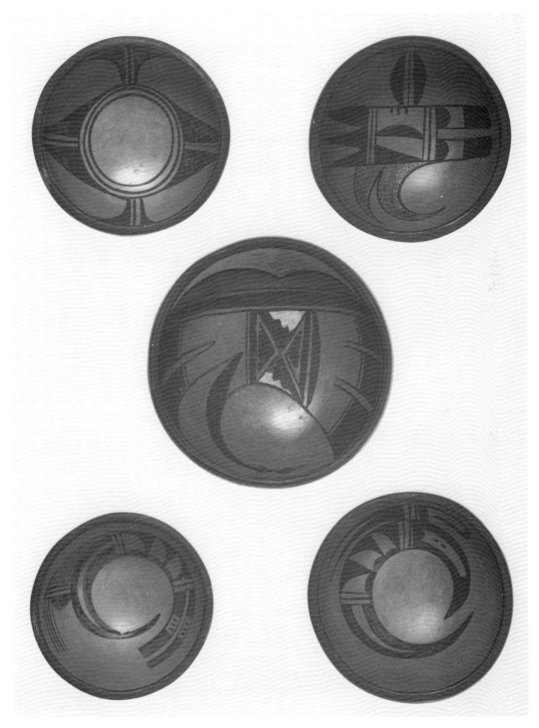

Plate 16. Polished Red Ware, bowls (Center bowl diameter at rim: 14.7 cm., all made by Ruth Takala)

115

Plate 17.   Polished Red Ware, bowl (Height: 8.8 cm., made by "Lucy's mother")

116

Plate 18. Polished Red Ware, tulip vases (Left vase height: 16.9 cm., made by Ruth Takala)

Plate 19. Polished Red Ware, tulip vases (Left vase height: 26.9 cm., made by Ethel Salyah, vase on right also made by Ethel Salyah and signed "Ethel")

118

Plate 20. Polished Red Ware, deep bowl (Height: 12.2 cm., made by Ethel Salyah)

Plate 21. Polished Red Ware, lamp (Height of jar utilized as the lamp base: 17.8 cm.)

120

Plate 22.   Polished Red Ware, miniatures ("Jar" in front height: 2.7 cm.)

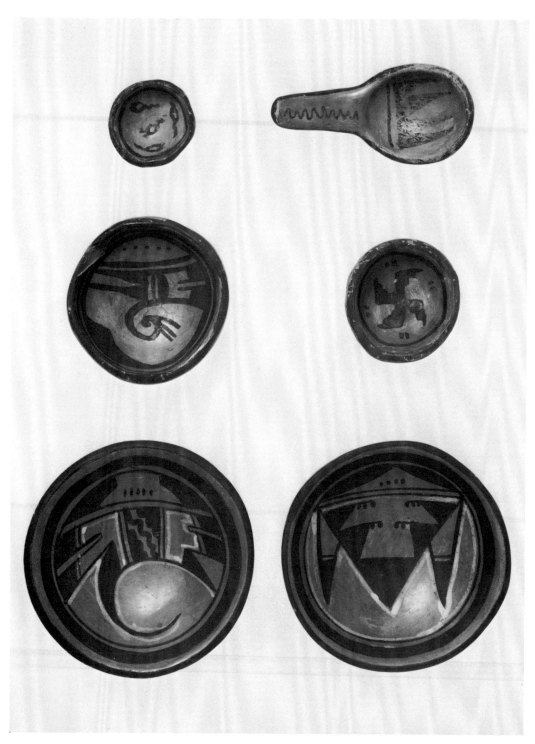

Plate 23. Polished Red Ware, miniatures (Ladle length: 9.0 cm.)

Plate 24.   Polished Red Ware (Right bowl height: 3.6 cm., made by "Maxie")

Plate 25. Polished Red Ware, plaque and bowl (Plaque diameter 15.9 cm., made by Ruth Takala)

Plate 26.   Unpolished Red Ware, bowl (Height: 10.4 cm.)

Plate 27.   Unpolished Red Ware, box (Base to rim height: 6.6 cm.)

Plate 28.   Unpolished Red Ware, doll's house and figurines (Total height: 13.7 cm.)

Plate 29. Red and Buff Ware (Left vessel height: 10.2 cm., made by Sellie. Mrs. Melville wrote the name on the base as "Sully", however, through the use of photographs it has been determined that this is the same person known as Sellie by members of the First Mesa Baptist Church.)

Plate 30. Red and Buff Ware, miniatures (Left bowl height: 3.5 cm.)

Plate 31. Red and Buff Ware, hats (Right cap length: 10.8 cm.)

130

Plate 32. Red and White Ware (Left vessel height: 10.0 cm., made by Ruth Takala. On each of the two vessels a given design occurs twice.)

131

Plate 33. Red and White Ware (Jar height: 19.7 cm., made by Sellie)

Plate 34.   Red and White Ware (Upper piece total length: 10.2 cm.)

Plate 35. White Ware (Top jar height: 19.2 cm., made by Sellie)

Plate 36. Brown Ware (Height 10.0 cm.)

Plate 37. Coiled Yucca and Woven Rabbit-brush Plaques (Lower left diameter: 28.8 cm.)

Plate 38. Coiled Yucca and Woven Rabbit-brush Baskets (Top basket height: 31.0 cm., interior of center right basket also illustrated in Plate 39)

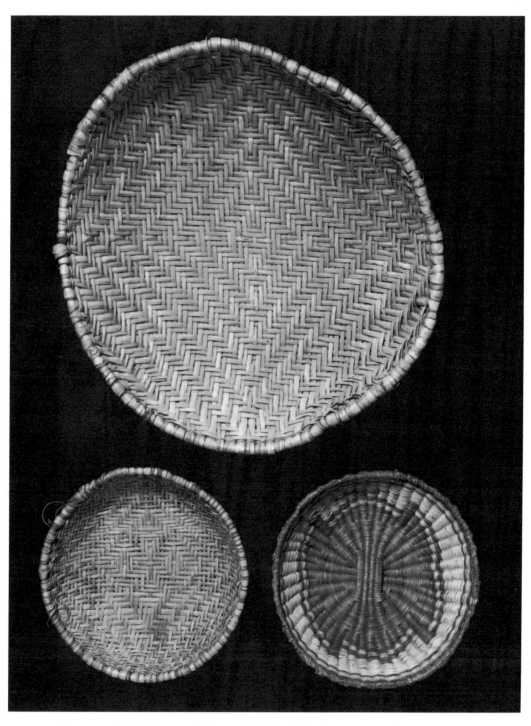

Plate 39. Plaited Yucca and Woven Rabbit-brush Baskets (Lower right woven Rabbit-brush basket diameter at rim: 26.0 cm.)

138

Plate 40.   Musical Instruments (Drum height: 18.0 cm.)

Plate 41.   Boys' and Men's Articles (Bow length: 63.5 cm.)

140

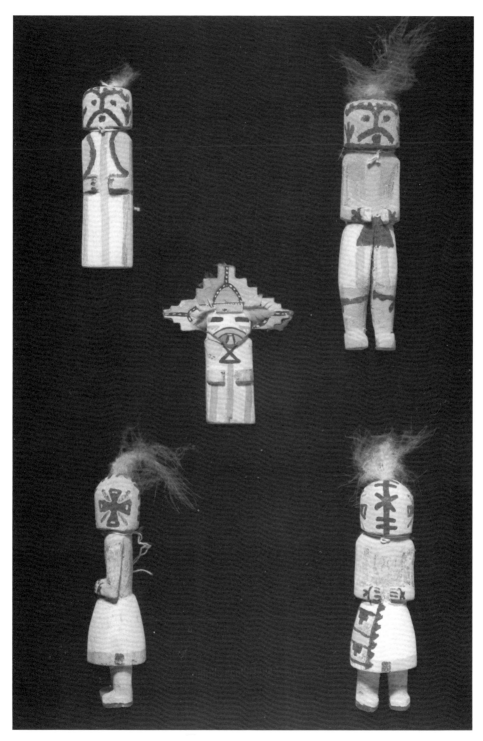

Plate 42. Kachina Dolls (Polik Mana, center, height: 9.9 cm.)

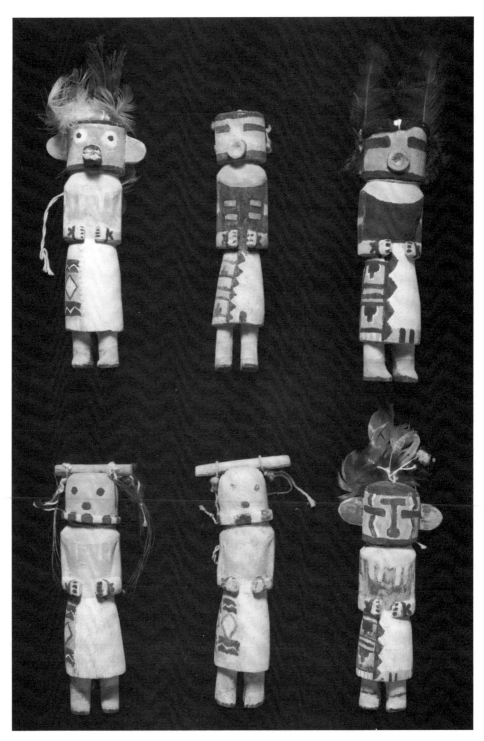

Plate 43. Kachina Dolls (Hakto Kachina, lower left, height: 16.6 cm.)

Plate 44. *Kachina Dolls (Umtoinaqa Kachina, lower far right, height: 18.5 cm.)*

143

Plate 45. Children's Toys Upper: Stuffed cloth dolls (Doll on left length: 32.0 cm.) Lower: Dolls and baby's gourd rattle (Kachina's cradle length: 21.0 cm.)

Plate 46.   Cottonwood Doll (Height: 26.4 cm., made by Hongavi)

Plate 47. Women's Clothes and Bride's Case

146

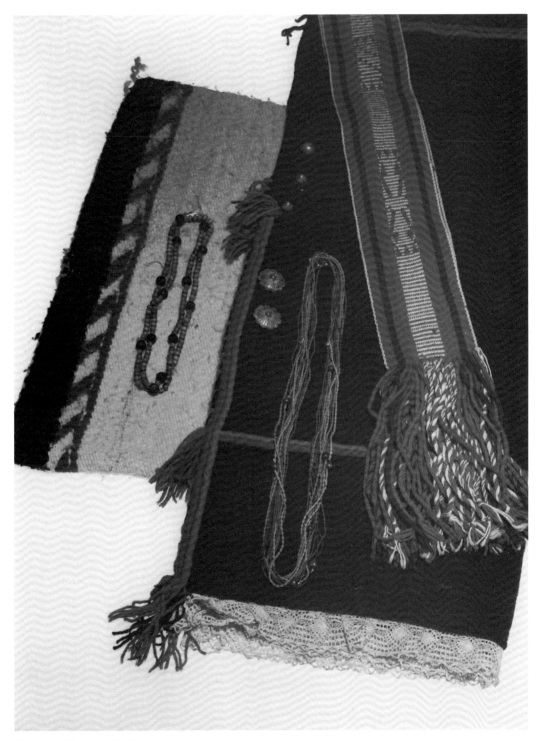

Plate 48. Women's Clothes

```
10% INTEREST ON ACCOUNTS OVERDUE
RAMAH TRADING CO.
GENERAL MERCHANDISE
                              7/5/29
Trading Post, Ramah, N. M.,              192
Name  Mrs. Carey E. Melville
      16 Isabella St., Worcester, M.
Sold by                    Forward

1  1 Navajo Bracelet          $5.00
2  2 pc. Zuni Pottery
      very old @ 50¢           1.00
   4 Navajo Silver Buttons
4        @ $1.00               4.00
5                            ---------
                             $10.00
6  Credit by check            10.00
7                            ---------
8                             00.00

9  Shipped in 2 pkgs. by insured
10 parcel post 7/5/29

11    Thanks for the order.
12
13
14
15  44
   Keep this slip. It is the only itemized bill you will receive.
        THE ADAMS BROS. CO. TOPEKA, KANS.
```

There have always been, and still are, a few Zuni potters who produce ceramics for sale (Wyckoff 1979); but the primary "art industry" of Zuni is silver-smithing, which was well established by 1873 (Walker 1974:72) and, by 1933, brought $30,000 into the pueblo (Wade 1976:93). But, although the Melvilles were interested in silverwork (White 1929b), it was pottery that they collected. Thus, in 1927, the Melvilles purchased a ceramic Zuni ashtray (Plate 49). What is most striking about this piece is that it has been decorated with the figure of a frog which, traditionally, was only sculptured on ceremonial vessels (Frank and Harlow 1974:Pl. XXX). This piece may well have been purchased at the Ramah Trading Company, adjacent to the Zuni reservation. While at this trading post Mrs. Melville admired some old Zuni pots and, nearly two years later, wrote requesting a vessel similar to one of the pieces she had seen earlier. In response to Mrs. Melville's request the trader, A. C. White, replied:

> . . . we are shipping the piece of pottery by express, certainly hope it reaches you in perfect condition, I'm very sorry, but we do not remember the exact piece that you have reference to or we might be able to almost duplicate same as we have a wonderful collection of Zuni pottery on hand at the present time, so we are selecting a piece which we certainly hope will be satisfactory and meet with your approval in every way (White 1929a).

Mrs. Melville was pleased with the choice made by the Ramah Trading Company. This piece (Plate 50) as well as another (Plate 51), which she also purchased from them, are now part of the Melville collection at Wesleyan.

The older of the two pieces (Plate 50) is an example of Kiapkwa Polychrome, which was made between 1760 and 1850. This bowl has extremely fine lines, as was commonly the case with early Kiapkwa Polychrome pieces. An early date for this piece is also indicated by the red rim, neck interior, and base, which, according to Frank and Harlow, was painted black after 1800 (Frank and Harlow 1974:137).

The large Zuni jar illustrated in Plate 51 is Kiapkwa in form. This jar form, a bulbous body on a restricted base surmounted by a wide neck and rim, continued, however, until 1900. The decoration on this piece is frequently referred to as a "rain bird" (Mera 1938) and is typical of Zuni Polychrome (1850–1900). It would seem to me, considering the form and decoration of this vessel as well as the manner in which the decoration is applied, that this piece is an early example of Zuni Polychrome. This style of decoration and the use of a white slip were adopted by the Hopis and appear in Polacca Polychrome after the famine of 1866–1867, which forced numbers of Hopis to take refuge at Zuni.

Other common motifs on Zuni Polychrome were small birds, sunflowers, and deer, shown with an arrow from mouth to heart. The Hopis utilized the bird and sunflower motifs, but only rarely the latter (Wade and McChesney 1981:234). This, however, was adopted by the Keres of both Acoma and Laguna Pueblos and is found on the pitcher from Laguna (Plate 52) purchased by the Melvilles in 1927.

Until around 1830 the pottery from Laguna is almost indistinguishable from that made at Acoma. Laguna Polychrome, which evolved from Acomita Polychrome, was produced from 1830 to 1930. The Laguna Polychrome pitcher in the Melville Collection is typical in its use of two tones of red and brownish black on a streaked white slip, as well as a red slip on the interior and on the concave base. Laguna Polychrome was widely sold to tourists during the 1880s, when the new Santa Fe Railroad traversed the village. After the First World War the station in the village was abandoned and the tracks were relocated to the north. This brought about a decline in ceramic production and the virtual abandonment of miniature and curio manufacture. Robert Gill (1976) has argued that it was partly as a result of this unstable commercial market that pottery never became a "tourist art" at Laguna, as it did at nearby Acoma. Furthermore, he notes that "the people of Laguna may have accepted the substitution of metal and china utensils and containers, but evidently there was no substitute for native-made jars, gift pots, or ceremonial bowls" (1976:113).

Gill's contention that Laguna pottery remained "traditional" in both its manufacture and use is of particular interest, because Laguna, as opposed to Zuni and Hopi, has been exposed to direct, alien pressure for over four hundred years. It was under Spanish religious and secular authority (Ellis 1959); and, when the United States annexed New Mexico, its policy of "civilizing" and "Christianizing" the Indians was implemented promptly at Laguna. At this time (1850) the majority of Lagunas were marginally Roman Catholic and, at the same time, were adherents of the Kachina cult. Medicine associations provided socio-political authority, the village chief himself coming from a specific medicine society rather than a specific clan, as at Hopi. These medicine societies proved critical to the Protestant missionaries. The missionary, Walter G. Marmon, who was also the government school teacher, married the village chief's daughter; and, as at Hopi, he dispensed western medicines. By combining the roles of school teacher, missionary, and medicine man, Walter Marmon and his brother gained considerable influence at Laguna. According to Spicer, their influence "was strong enough that each was chosen at different times to be governor of the village" (Spicer 1962:177); however, factionalism developed. In 1880 the more conservative group moved to Isleta, leaving at Laguna a population eager to gain a cash income either from wage labor or from the tourist market. This group, however, never totally abandoned their old religion or the manufacture and use of traditional pottery types (Spicer 1962:178).

The group that moved to Isleta, a Tiwa pueblo south of Albuquerque, founded a satellite village called Oraibi. The name of the village makes one wonder whether traditional Hopis married to Lagunas were not part of the group. This immigrant population took with them the Laguna style of pottery.

The similarities between Laguna and Isleta pottery can be seen by comparing the two vessels from these pueblos found in the Melville collection. The Isleta bowl (Plate 53), like the vessel from Laguna, is slipped red on the interior and white on the exterior. The design likewise utilizes right-angle triangles, groups of multiple brownish black lines, and two tones of red. The pigments differ because different sources were used. This is also true of the white slip. Different clay sources are also indicated by the color variation, pinkish, as opposed to buff, and the presence or absence of mica. The forms of Isleta bowls are similar to those of Laguna except that the concave bases, which have persisted at Laguna, were replaced at Isleta by flat ones.

Like the potters at Laguna, the Isleta potters manufactured miniatures and curios for sale to tourists at their railway station. Also, both pueblos later, in the 1920s and 1930s, had the advantage of being located on major highways. It was along these roads that the Melvilles travelled.

Plate 49. Zuni Ashtray, c. 1927 (Height: 2.6 cm.)

Plate 50. Kiapkwa Polychrome (Height: 16.0 cm.)

Plate 51. Zuni Polychrome (Height 27.5 cm.)

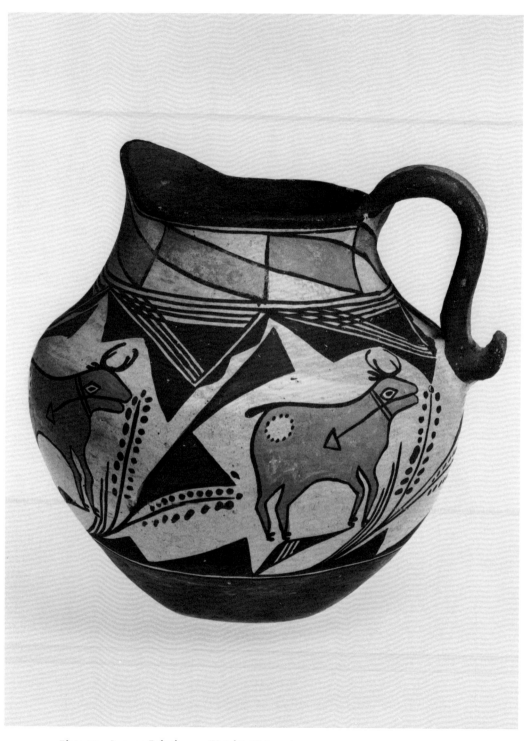

Plate 52. Laguna Polychrome (Height: 18.4 cm.)

154

Plate 53. Isleta Bowl, c. 1927 (Height: 9.8 cm.)

RIO GRANDE
TEWA

Mission church at San Ildefonso Pueblo—1978 (Photograph by Lydia L. Wyckoff)

When the Melville family visited the Tewa pueblos just north of Santa Fe they felt that they were classified as tourists and that the potters were only interested in money. (See Chapter 1.) This is not surprising. During the course of the preceding four hundred years, the Tewas had been forced to adapt to a foreign presence. In the process they incorporated Spanish religious and political elements into their indigenous religious and socio-political systems (Ortiz 1969). The adaptation of these foreign elements permitted them to function within the larger, dominant and often oppressive socio-economic system while maintaining their ethnic identity.

As part of the Spanish socio-economic system, Tewa ceramics have long been produced as a commercial item. Nambe manufactured polychrome wares for the Spaniards and Mexicans until 1830 (Frank and Harlow 1974: 39–40). By 1880, however, both Nambe and Tesuque manufactured only culinary wares for local use. San Ildefonso, which had not produced much pottery for the Spanish market, began to manufacture ceramics for the American tourist trade after the railroad was built in 1882. San Ildefonso Polychrome continued to be made from the 1880s until about 1910. "Pottery trinkets" were also produced for the tourist trade (Chapman 1970:23–24).

In contrast to these more southern Tewa pueblos are Santa Clara and San Juan. Because they were located farther from Santa Fe, pottery was not manufactured for the Spanish population at these pueblos and polychrome wares were not produced after 1700 (Frank and Harlow 1974:29). After this date and until the 1900s only black and brown pottery was made. The difference between these wares is caused by different firing techniques and not by the color of the slip or clay. The black pottery was, and still is today, fired in a reducing atmosphere, in which little air is allowed to enter so that smoke surrounds each piece, turning it black. When the piece is fired brown, air is allowed to enter; thus, the smoke is removed and the piece is not blackened. Between the late eighteenth century and the early twentieth century, only black ware was produced at Santa Clara. The glossy finish of these vessels appealed to tourists in the 1880s. One of the distinctive features of Santa Clara pottery (Plate 54) was the rippled or fluted rim or neck (Frank and Harlow 1974:30). Sculptured embellishments, specifically the bear's paw, were occasionally added after 1880.

Brown ware was primarily produced at San Juan. Occasionally, however, a piece might be fired black. One San Juan diagnostic is that the slip is applied to only about two thirds of the vessel. Sometime in the 1920s San Juan potters began incising their vessels. On the bowl illustrated in Plate 55 the design areas are edged with incising and then filled with white or red. This is an early example of San Juan Polychrome.

It is beyond the scope of these notes to attempt to unravel the complex American and Tewa socio-economic forces which led to the failure of the 1880 San Ildefonso ceramic revival. Critical, however, was the decline in sales of large San Ildefonso Polychrome pieces, apparently resulting from the Anglo American recession of 1893 and economic conditions preceding and during the First World War. Anglo buyers were fewer and were unwilling to spend very much for a piece of pottery; also tourists wanted small, portable pieces. Furthermore, tourists and traders may have felt that some of these pieces were poorly made. With tourists and traders offering very little cash for pottery, Tewa potters, acutely aware of the American "hourly wage" concept, began seeking ways in which to decrease the time expended on making pottery. It was apparently for this reason that the potters of San Ildefonso abandoned the white San Ildefonso Polychrome slip for that imported from Cochiti, a nearby Keresan pueblo. The San Ildefonso Polychrome slip was stone polished, whereas the Cochiti slip was only wiped, thus saving many hours of labor. The use of this slip had become widespread by 1910.

The vessel in Plate 56 utilizes the Cochiti slip, which tends to be grayer and grainier on vessels made at San Ildefonso than on those of Cochiti. The variance in this slip has been explained by the San Ildefonso potters' failure to master its use and the suggestion that Cochiti exported inferior materials (Frank and Harlow 1974:36). Be this as it may, the vessel in the Melville Collection (Plate 56) was probably made at San Ildefonso, as the slip is a brown-gray and grainy and the design is not typical of Cochiti.

At the close of the First World War Kenneth Chapman and Wesley Bradfield of the School of American Research set about rejuvenating and preserving Tewa pottery. Their goals were similar to those formulated fifteen years later by the Museum of Northern Arizona. Like the Museum of Northern Arizona, they were concerned about the poor quality of pottery. At this time dealers bought pottery by the lot, not the piece, and simply discarded that which they considered unmarketable. In 1919 the School of American Research adopted the following policy:

1. Inviting the potters to submit their wares to us at the Museum before offering them for sale elsewhere.
2. Asking each potter to set her price, piece by piece.
3. Selecting a few outstanding pieces, if any, and explaining why they were chosen (for form, finish, decoration, etc.).
4. Adding at least 25 percent to the price named by the potter for those selected, and promising still higher prices for further improvements.
5. Explaining that selected pieces would be sold at the Museum at a markup sufficient only to repay the school for the time devoted to the project by Bradfield and [Chapman] (Chapman 1970:28).

The first potters to bring in a "wagonload of their pottery" were Maria and Julian Martinez of San Ildefonso, who were already considered master craftsmen at that time. They produced "Tunyo Polychrome," i.e., San Ildefonso Polychrome with a Cochiti slip, until shortly before 1920. Chapman attributes the "invention" of matte painting on a polished surface to Julian Martinez in 1919 (Frank and Harlow 1974:34). Two things, however, should be pointed out. Firstly, it is both technically and esthetically a fusion of Santa Clara Black Ware and the San Ildefonso painted ceramic tradition, since the designs on Black-on-Black Ware were painted on the polished vessel surface prior to firing. Secondly, this ware, which is stone polished, would probably not have been developed had the School of American Research not emphasized and subsidized technical excellence.

There are three Black-on-Black pieces in the Melville Collection. The bird dish (Plate 57) is simply signed "Marie." This signature, pressed into the clay base with a smooth instrument, probably a polishing stone, was used by Maria from approximately 1923 until around 1925 (Harlow 1977:36). As the bird dish was bought by the Melvilles in 1927, it may be either that Maria was sufficiently successful that she could defer sales until her price was met or that she continued to use this signature occasionally. There is little doubt, however, that by 1927 the Martinez family had already achieved widespread recognition. The School of American Research had succeeded in raising prices and educating the public as to the value of Indian arts, and was instrumental in establishing the Santa Fe Indian Fair, at which Maria had won a number of prizes. The Black-on-Black pottery was extremely popular, so popular, in fact, that Maria and Julian were unable to "supply even a fraction of the demand" (Wade 1976:162). This led to the development of specialization and a modified production line:

> By the end of the 1920's [Maria] had devised a new method for increasing production. Several of her relatives were hired to assist her in the various stages of pottery manufacturing (Wade 1976:162).

The Black-on-Black "wedding vase" (Plate 58) is signed "Maria & Julian" which is cut into the clay base with a pencil. According to Harlow (1977:36) this signature was used from around 1925 until Julian's death in 1943. Evidently, however, it is not commonly found on pieces made before 1934 (Anonymous 1974:86). Thus it may be that this vessel was not purchased until after the Melvilles' visit in 1927, possibly when they returned to the Southwest in 1934.

During the Tewa ceramic revival of the 1920s polychrome was being produced at San Juan (Plate 55) and Black Ware at San Ildefonso. Shapes became more varied. Some, like the bird vessel (Plate 57) were innovative, whereas others, like the wedding vase (Plate 58) were now made in all the pottery producing Tewa pueblos. Originally the wedding vase was associated with Santa Clara, the only pueblo where it is still used for ceremonial purposes (Harlow 1977:30). The spread of this vessel form is attributed to its commercial success; it was introduced to First Mesa in the 1930s.

Ceramic plates (Plate 59) were also made. Some were decorated solely with the matte black paint, whereas others were carved. The plate in the Melville Collection is decorated with an *avanyu* or plumed serpent. This figure was frequently used by Julian (Harlow 1977:36); but the plate is signed "Isabel." The *avanyu* on this piece is carved and scraped into the surface as well as painted on. According to Chapman (1970:35) the carving is done prior to slipping and polishing. This piece, like the wedding vase, may likewise have been bought after the Melvilles' 1927 visit, as this technique of decoration is believed to have been developed in 1929 by Rose Gonzales (Anonymous 1974:79). If these vessels were indeed purchased after 1927, it may be that the Tewas succeeded in making the Melvilles into long term tourist/traders despite their initial, negative reaction in 1927.

Plate 54.   Santa Clara Black Ware, bowls (Top bowl height: 18.5 cm.)

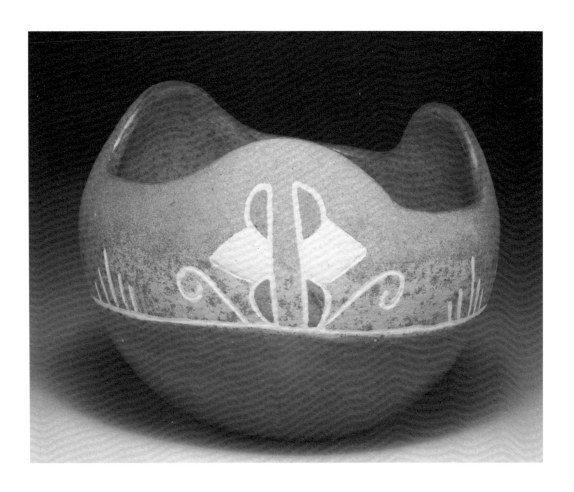

Plate 55.   San Juan Polychrome (Height: 12.0 cm.)

Plate 56.   *Tunyo Polychrome (Maximum height: 12.4 cm.)*

162

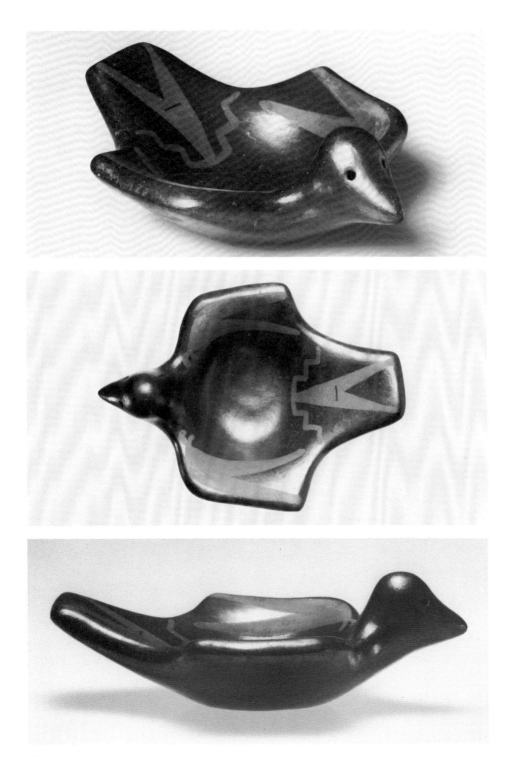

Plate 57. Black-on-Black Ware, bowl (Length: 18.5 cm., signed "Marie")

Plate 58. Black-on-Black Ware, wedding vase (Height: 20.8 cm., signed "Marie & Julian")

Plate 59. Black-on-Black Ware, plate (Diameter: 24.0 cm., signed "Isabel")

NAVAJO
and
PIMA

Navajo dolls made for the tourist trade—1927

Navajo women were recognized as master weavers in 1927, as they are today. Unlike their pueblo neighbors, they did not weave prior to the introduction of sheep by the Spaniards, at which time the Navajos were hunters and gatherers. The first reference to the Navajos, as distinct from their Apache cousins, is in 1626 when they were referred to as "Apaches of Navaju" (Spicer 1962:211). At about this time the Navajos changed their economic base to pastoralism supplemented by horticulture and gathering. Although the Spanish government attempted to settle the Navajos in villages and convert them to the Roman Catholic faith, their efforts failed; and, being free from Spanish control, the Navajos offered a sanctuary to Pueblo peoples fleeing Spanish oppression. After the Pueblo Revolt of 1680 many pueblo Indians took refuge with the Navajos. According to Amsden (1934:129), the Navajos learned weaving from these Pueblo refugees.

By 1799 woven Navajo goods had become important trade items and were exchanged for Pueblo corn and fruit (Amsden 1934:133). The most prized and widely traded item was the man's shoulder blanket, also referred to as a "chief's blanket," not because it was a badge of chieftanship but because to possess one indicated affluence. These early shoulder blankets, as well as women's shoulder blankets and dresses, were black and decorated with stripes of blue and later red. Black wool was dyed with sumac to create a more even color; and white wool was dyed blue with imported indigo. The red yarn was obtained by Spain from England and then exported to the New World. The Navajo blanket was, therefore, on the one hand an indigenous trade item and, on the other, a product of international trade. Thus the Navajos made a blanket that was uniquely their own, using an acquired yarn, be it from baze or sheep, an acquired skill, that of weaving, acquired dyes, and, initially, the parallel stripe design of Pueblo weavers.

Navajo weaving flourished. Red baize or bayeta was extensively used between 1850 and 1863, but continued to be imported after the Navajos came under American military control (Amsden 1934:141). Designs became more complex, with stepped pyramids and serrated triangles possibly derived from Mexican *serapes*.

The military defeat of the Navajo in 1864 and their subsequent incarceration on government rations had an enormous impact; and the Navajos who were permitted to go home four years later were never to be quite the same people that made "the long walk" in 1864 to Bosque Redondo. During their captivity they acquired a taste for coffee, sugar, and flour; and they were issued machine-spun Saxony yarn (Dedera 1975:28).

From this time on the trader became a key figure in the development of Navajo weaving; and Navajo blankets became, once again, one of their primary trade items. Until around 1890 however, the majority of Navajo blankets were poorly woven and made of Germantown yarn and a cotton warp. Yarn from Germantown, Pennsylvania, was aniline dyed. Aniline dyes soon became "typical" of Navajo weaving. The traders sold packaged dyes, Germantown yarn, and cotton warp thread to the Navajos and other trade goods, including Pendleton blankets, in return for Navajo weaving (McNitt 1962:222). As blankets could now be woven more rapidly, the number of blankets woven increased to meet the demand of the tourist trade, which reached the Southwest with the railroad.

The early tourists may not have demanded technical skill, but they did want something that looked "Indian" and would be appropriate back home. In order to meet the former requirement, arrow and swastika designs were introduced; and, in order to become an American household item, the blanket became a rug. As a rug, the Navajo blanket was now bordered in accordance with American taste. It soon became apparent that the cotton warp, introduced by the traders, rapidly deteriorated when given the wear of a rug. Traders, therefore, ceased supplying cotton warp and, in an effort to rejuvenate the now sagging Navajo rug market, stopped buying rugs by the pound and began to pay higher prices for better woven rugs. They also encouraged designs which had proven to be popular. It is said that J. B. Moore, the trader at Crystal in the Chuska mountains between 1896 and 1911, obtained linoleum samples to serve as patterns for Navajo weavers (McNitt 1962:252–256). The rug illustrated in Plate 60 is probably from this area, as indicated by the block-like triangles, possibly derived from Moore's linoleum blocks, as well as the little crooks added to the base of two of the triangles. This rug may have been ten or fifteen years old when purchased by the Melvilles in 1927. Like the other two rugs in the Melville collection, it has what are called "lazy lines." These diagonal lines can be more clearly seen in the Crystal rug. See, for example, the upper left corner, where the background consists of a variety of dark wools ranging from black to brown. Lazy lines are created when the weft is not woven across the entire warp, but only to the farthest point easily reached by the weaver without changing her position. The presence of these lazy lines in the Crystal Style rug indicates that, although stripes (reminiscent of early nineteenth century blankets) are formed by the different wools, the black area was conceived of as "background" for the white design. This, along with the border, identifies this piece unequivocally as a rug made for the American market.

The two rugs in Plate 61 were probably new when bought by the Melvilles in 1927. These rugs, made like the former one of "homespun" wool, are what James (1914:149–151) terms "Standard Rugs." The red and black portions have been dyed with aniline dyes. The jagged edges of the triangles and the vertical border of the lower rug are, however, associated with the Gallup area.

In 1927, rugs usually conformed to the regional standards of the area in which they were made, and were classified accordingly. Rugs made for Moore's Crystal Trading Post, for example, were called "Crystal" rugs. Rugs made for Lorenzo Hubbel's Ganado Trading Post, which emphasized diamonds on a red background, were known as Ganado rugs. The rug illustrated in Plate 61 (lower) is similar to this type and has the double frame characteristic of the Ganado Style. The Gallup area was known for its pictorials, especially rugs featuring cornstalks. Such a rug is illustrated in Plate 62 (lower). Pictorial rugs depicting anything from *hogans* to trains have occasionally been produced on the Navajo Reservation since the 1890s. Rugs depicting *Yeis*, the supernatural beings of the Navajos, were not made until sometime after 1900. It is said that weavers were induced to make these rugs by Will

Evans of the Shiprock Trading Company (Dedera 1975:68). According to James (1914:139) the first *yei* rug was greeted with "shocked surprise, thrilled horror and fierce condemnation from the Navajos," who were violently opposed to the portrayal of these sacred figures. James states that, all over the reservation, councils were held and that the trader's life was threatened. The weaver of this rug had, according to James (1914:140), felt free to depict these figures, "having lost the superstitious fear that oppresses most Navajos." One can but wonder if this weaver, like some of the Hopi–Tewa Sikyatki Revival potters, had not become a Christian. This first rug was sold for "several hundred dollars" (James 1914:140). In 1914, it is thought that only six or seven of these rugs existed. In 1934, however, Amsden wrote that:

> The *Yei* blanket is becoming more and more common. Certain traders seem to encourage its manufacture because they can sell it for a good price by playing up its rarity and pseudoceremonial character. Evidently the Navajo themselves regard the *Yei* blanket much as we would consider a parody of the Bible, as something in bad taste (1934:106).

The *Yei* rug in the Melville collection was probably purchased at this time (1934) and not during their 1927 trip. The brilliant aniline colors used for all but the white and gray, have not faded. The Melvilles used this piece as a wall hanging. *Yei* rugs are not bordered and are, perhaps, more properly considered as hangings. The use of Navajo rugs as wall hangings became popular in the late 1920s and 1930s, for Navajo rugs were by then considered "works of art" and not simply tourist items.

After leaving Polacca the Melvilles visited Sunset Crater and continued south, toward Tucson, before turning west to California. In the Gila Valley they purchased for 35 cents, a small pot (Plate 63) made by the Pimas. Between 1849 and 1878 the Pimas had supplied food for travellers to the west coast; wagon trains bound for California stopped to resupply their food stores from the abundant crops raised by the Pimas along the Gila river (Spicer 1962:147). In 1927, however, the Pimas could offer travellers little more than craft work. They were unable to irrigate their lands after 1887, when the river was diverted to irrigate Anglo American farms. It was probably here that the Melvilles purchased two Pima baskets (Plate 63). These are woven from willow, with Devil's Claw used for the black design. The smaller of these two baskets was probably made at the time of the Melville's visit in 1927 and, like the ceramic pot, was made for the tourist trade. The larger basket appears, however, to be older, possibly dating from the early 1900s. This basket may have been purchased by the Melvilles but it may also have been acquired earlier by Mrs. Melville's father.

Plate 60. Navajo Rug in the Crystal Style (Length: 148.0 cm.)

Plate 61. *Navajo Standard Rugs (Upper length: 170.0 cm.; lower length: 129.0 cm.)*

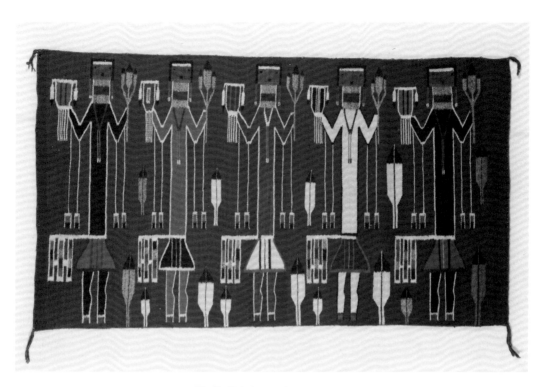

Plate 62. Navajo Rugs (Yei rug length: 171.5 cm.; corn stalk pictorial rug length: 141.0 cm.)

Plate 63.   Pima Baskets and Pottery Bowl (Lower basket height: 9.7 cm.)

PLAINS
and
PLATEAU
PEOPLES

*Nineteenth century Plains
Indian quirt of horsehair
woven around a rawhide core.*

Plains Indian beadwork is a clear and at times painful document of culture change. The development of eighteenth and early nineteenth century Plains culture was based on bison hunting made economically feasible through the non-indigenous horse. The people of the Plains, like the Navajo, had the ability to incorporate imported items and truly make them their own, as with the horse and the trade bead. Prior to 1800 most decoration was either painted or embroidered with seeds or porcupine quills. Since porcupines are not native to much of the plains area, these were probably acquired through trade. The Teton Dakotas had moved onto the plains from their eastern prairie fringe around 1750 and, therefore, were not drawn into the European fur trade. The more eastern Yanktons, however, were the "middlemen" between the traders and the Tetons. In return for horses they distributed guns, ammunition and other local items, including, perhaps, forest porcupine quills, which may have been acquired in turn from the Ojibwas. After 1800 "pony beads," so called because they were exchanged for Indian ponies, were also traded (Hail 1980:51). Traded porcupine quills decorate the upper fringe area of the Dakota style pipe bag in Plate 64. The beadwork on this bag, however, is done in "seed beads," so termed because they were similar in size to the seeds which they had replaced. Seed beads became widely used after 1840, replacing large pony beads for embroidery, although old pony beads were still occasionally used (Plate 65:upper right).

Plains trade also extended westward to the Plateau region. The Nez Perces and Flatheads played an important role in the western trade, exchanging dentalia and other valuables from the coast for buffalo robes and horses. Spencer and Jennings (1977:167) have argued that slaves from the northwest coast were also critical "trade items." The primary link between the plains and the northwest coast was the Columbia River. Trading and other social activities occurred at various fishing stations. The Nez Perces, like other Plateau ethnic groups, relied on salmon as a primary food source, often, it is said, spearing salmon from horseback. Along with the horse, the Nez Perces adopted horse trappings and bags and pouches which would lie flat against the animal. A Nez Perce pouch is illustrated in Plate 67. This pouch is similar in shape to those of the Plains peoples, but it is made of Indian hemp rather than hide, and decorated with wool rather than beads. The design is in the Central Plains geometric style of the late 1800s. Wool was acquired through Anglo traders or missionaries.

Baskets of the type illustrated at the top and center of Plate 68 are commonly referred to as "Salish" (Rozaire 1977:7). The use of this general linguistic term reflects the fact that such groups as the Thompsons, the Sanpoil, etc. were much alike in culture and technology as well as in language. These two baskets, the uppermost being a drinking cup, probably date from around the turn of the century as basket bases were introduced into the area by the missionaries. The lower basket in Plate 68 can be identified as of Klikitat manufacture by the scallop above the rim (Conn 1979:249). The Klikitat lived in the lower Columbia valley.

The Flatheads, like the Nez Perces, acquired horses from the plains. Toward the close of the nineteenth century they also adopted beadwork. A pouch dating from the turn of the century is illustrated in Plate 65, lower row, left. The primary stimulus for the diffusion of this floral style of beadwork was United States policy and the missionaries, not indigenous trade.

Because of intertribal marriages and warfare, it is often extremely difficult to determine the tribal origin of a specific piece of beadwork. Many groups did, however, during diverse periods develop distinctive styles. The two bags in Plate 65, upper left and center, are examples of Cheyenne beadwork. The "stripe style" (Hail 1980:59) seen here was most popular with the Cheyennes during the pony bead period (1800–1840), but it continued to be used until approximately 1860. The moccasins in Plate 66, lower right, are also probably Cheyenne, although possibly of a somewhat later date.

It is difficult to determine the tribal origin of items made after about 1860 in the Plains and Plateau regions. Under ever increasing pressure from American settlers and the military, the various tribal bands joined together to resist the common enemy. After the massacre of Cheyennes at Sand Creek in 1864 and the subsequent investigations which made known the atrocities committed by U.S. soldiers, public opinion was aroused in favor of a peace policy. This policy, which supported the maintenance of reservations to protect the Americans and Indians from each other, held that, if Christianized and educated, Indians could, in fact, become citizens. Thus, as bitter warfare swept through nearly all the Plains tribes during the four years that followed the Sand Creek massacre, missionaries prepared to enter this area. In 1868 a treaty was concluded with the Dakotas and Cheyennes at Fort Laramie. This treaty, like the preceding treaties, did not bring about the cessation of warfare. This was not to come until 1877. Stands in Timber, a Cheyenne, recollected how, at that time, General Nelson A. Miles, the commanding officer at Fort Keogh, told the Cheyenne leaders that:

> The government would fulfill its agreement made in the Treaty of 1868, and build them houses and give them equipment for farming and gardening, so they could begin to live like white men.

> The Cheyenne finally agreed . . . . when the people got in, they were issued tents and stoves and other things, . . . and [the United States army] took their guns and horses. For the first time the Cheyenne became a surrendered, captive people (Stands In Timber and Liberty 1967:224–225).

During this period of conflict and early captivity, regional styles reflecting military alliances developed. The "Central Style" was shared by the Cheyennes, Dakotas and Arapahos of South Dakota, southern Montana and Wyoming. According to Hail (1980:59), "Teton beadworkers were the most prolific on the Plains" and it was they who "created the Central Plains style." This style uses the "lazy stitch" in which about ten beads are strung and sewed down at the ends. White or blue beads were used for the background and the geometric figures were usually executed in blue, green, yellow and white. The Teton Dakota style pipe bag (Plate 64: left) illustrates the Central Plains style. Other examples are the bag in Plate 65 (upper right) and the two pairs of moccasins in Plate 66 (right center and lower). These pieces all use the Bohemian bead, which was widely traded after 1870.

The upper pair of moccasins in Plate 66 are clearly Teton Dakota. After 1870 these people developed a more elaborate style in which geometric forms frequently end in a hook or fork. Hail argues that "in this time of confinement to the reservation and ever present frustration, the response of the women seems to have been to keep their hands and minds occupied, and they entered their most prolific period of beadwork" (1980:59).

The Central Plains geometric style is distinct from the floral style of the Plains Crees and Ojibwas, which developed in the Great Lakes area out of prehistoric curvilinear designs after the arrival of Europeans. The Ojibwas expanded westward with the fur trade, and some of them reached the Plains in the nineteenth century as the Dakotas and Cheyennes had done before them. Like the other Plains societies, they beaded portable objects, such as pipe bags (Plate 64: right) and pouches (Plate 65: lower row, third from left). Both of these pieces utilize the overlay bead stitch. This technique consists of stringing the desired number of beads and then placing them on the article to be decorated in either a straight or curved line; a second thread secures the beads with a tiny stitch at intervals of from one to four beads.

Unless documented, Cree and Ojibwa beadwork cannot be distinguished. Both groups used the overlay stitch and floral designs. The background is either white or blue; and the figures are outlined with either a single or double row of beads which create shading. Floral designs spread rapidly throughout the northern and central plains during the latter half of the nineteenth century, carried by Indians, no doubt, who were being concentrated on reservations and in boarding schools in that period. The Rocky Boy Reservation in Montana became the center of the Cree and Ojibwa style, which was adopted by the adjacent Flatheads and Crows, who simplified the units and utilized a rigid bilateral layout, converting the Cree-Ojibwa curvilinear designs into geometric patterns. A calico-lined pouch of this type is illustrated in Plate 65 (lower left). This piece is probably Flathead, to judge from its light blue background and three flower symmetry (in this example three leaves), large simple forms, contour beading and outlining (Hail 1980:65).

Floral designs were also adopted by the Cheyennes who, unlike the Crees and Ojibwas, did not usually bead the background. Some of these pieces, like the Flathead piece, clearly use floral forms within a geometric frame. Other pieces in this style are similar to work produced after 1860 by Indians "removed" to Indian Territory. It is possible that the Northern Cheyennes, who were moved to Oklahoma Territory in 1877 and who fought their way home through the U.S. Army a year later, brought this style back to the Dakota-Cheyenne area.

The popularity and wide distribution of floral designs make it impossible to determine the makers of the small bag and heart-shaped frame in the Melville collection. The design on the frame has been drawn in ink prior to beading, implying Anglo tutelage. Comparison of the large stitches, which are in plain sight on the front of the frame, with the fine stitching which binds the beads to the frame and is concealed by the beads, indicates a lack of understanding of both the purpose and the process of Anglo tacking. Across the top is written "Aline May 9."

In 1879 boarding schools were established in the hope that they would both Christianize and "civilize" the Indians. Bead weaving was taught, and sometimes applied to new items. Compare the "traditional" design in Plate 66 (lower left) with the bookmark in Plate 65 (lower right).

All of this beadwork, and the baskets and Nez Perce bag, were collected by Mrs. Melville's father. A daughter of Mrs. Melville, Martha Melville Fletcher, believes that her grandfather acquired it through a fellow minister who was a missionary. If this is the case, missionaries have not only been bearers of American culture but have also served to disseminate Plains and Plateau material culture, not to mention the Hopi material acquired by the Melvilles in 1927. It was probably in 1927 that the woven bead belt and head bands (Plate 66: left) were purchased. They feature bright Japanese beads and are not at all in keeping with the earlier Plains-Plateau material.

Plate 64. Plains Indian Beadwork, pipe bags (Left bag length: 96.0 cm.)

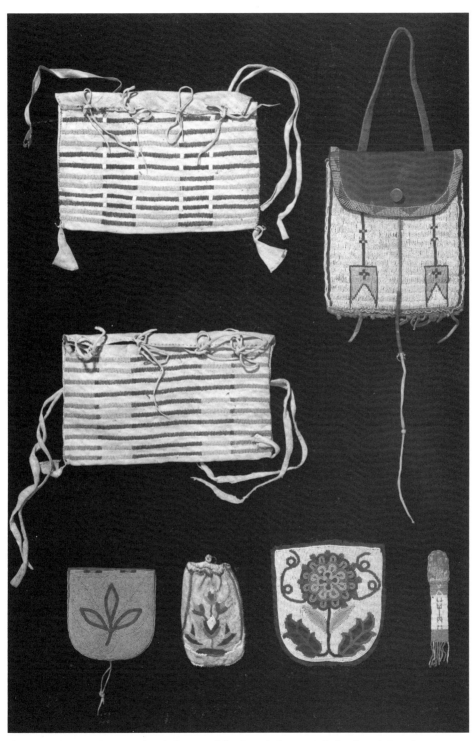

Plate 65. Plains Indian Beadwork, bags and bookmark (Lower right bookmark length: 17.0 cm.)

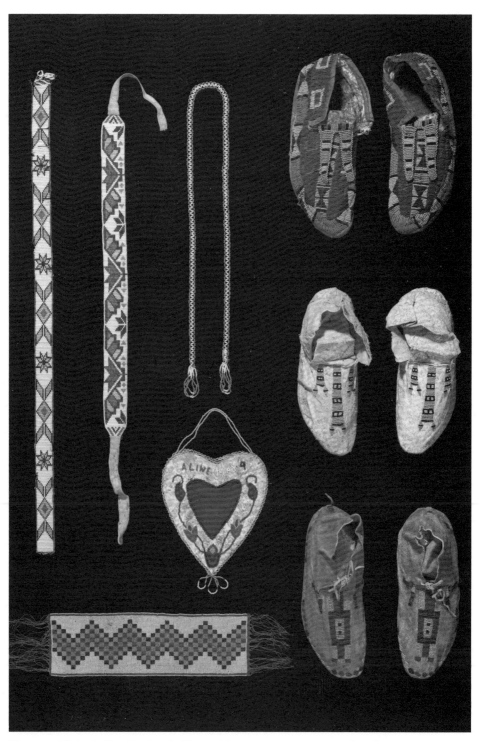

Plate 66. *Plains Indian Beadwork (Upper right moccassins maximum length: 25.7 cm.)*

Plate 67.   Nez Perce Pouch (Length: 26.8 cm.)

Plate 68. Salish and Klikitat Baskets (The lower basket is Klikitat. Height at maximum point: 7.4 cm.)

REFERENCES

Amsden, Charles Avery
  1934   *Navaho Weaving: its Technic and History*. The Fine Arts Press, Santa Ana.

Anonymous
  1974   *Seven Families in Pueblo Pottery*. University of New Mexico Press, Albuquerque.
  1978   *The Hopi and Navajo Shows at the Museum of Northern Arizona—Show Policies and Procedures 12/1/78.*
  1982   *Hopi Show Museum of Northern Arizona July 3–7, 1982* (announcement circulated by mail).

Barilli, Renato
  1969   *Art Nouveau*. Hamlyn Publishing Group Ltd., London.

Bartlett, Katharine
  1936   "How to appreciate Hopi handicrafts," Museum Notes 9.1, Museum of Northern Arizona, Flagstaff.
  1977   "A History of Hopi pottery," *Plateau* 49.3: 2–23.

Beadle, J. H.
  1878   *Western Wilds, and the Men who Redeem Them; An Authentic Narrative*. Jones Bros. & Co., Cincinnati.

Bloom, L. B.
  1931   "A Campaign against the Moqui Pueblos," *New Mexico Historical Review* 6.2:158–226.
  1936   "Bourke on the Southwest," *New Mexico Historical Review* 11:217–282.

Bourke, John G.
  1884   *The Snake Dance of the Moquis of Arizona*. Sampson, Low, Marston, Searle and Rivington, London.

Breunig, Robert G.
  1978   "Museum interpretation," *Plateau* 50.4:8–11.

Bunzel, Ruth
  1929   *The Pueblo Potter*. Columbia University, Press, New York, reprinted Dover Publications, New York, 1972.

Calhoun, James S.
  1915   *The Official Correspondence of James S. Calhoun*. Bureau of Indian Affairs, Government Printing Office, Washington, D. C.

Carlson, Vada F.
  1964   *No Turning Back*. University of New Mexico Press, Albuquerque.

Chapman, Kenneth M.
  1970   *The Pottery of San Ildefonso Pueblo*. School of American Research Monograph Series, no. 28, Santa Fe.

Clemmer, Richard O.
1977 "The Alienating effects of industrialization and political reorganization on Hopi society," *Southwest Economy and Society* 2.
1978 *Continuities of Hopi Culture Change.* Acoma Books, Ramona.

Collier, John
1936 "Meeting with the Hopis at Oraibi, April 7, 1936, MS., National Archives, Hopi Files.
1963 *From Every Zenith: A Memoir.* Sage Books, Denver.

Collins, John E.
1974 *Nampeyo, Hopi Potter.* Muckenthaler Cultural Center, Fullerton.

Colton, Mary-Russell
1938 "The Arts and crafts of the Hopi Indians: their historic background, processes and methods of manufacture and the work of the museum for the maintenance of Hopi arts," Museum Notes 11.3, Museum of Northern Arizona, Flagstaff.

Conn, Richard
1979 *Native American Art in the Denver Art Museum.* University of Washington Press, Seattle.

Connelly, John C.
1979 "Hopi social organization," *Handbook of North American Indians* vol. 9 (Southwest), pp. 539–553, Alfonso Ortiz, volume editor, W. C. Sturtevant, general editor, Smithsonian Institution, Washington, D. C.

Crane, Leo
1925 *Indians of the Painted Desert.* Little, Brown & Co., Boston.

Curtis, Natalie
1907 *The Indians' Book.* Harper, New York.

Dedera, Don
1975 *Navajo Rugs.* Northland Press, Flagstaff.

Dockstader, Frederick J.
1954 *The Kachina and the White man: A study of the Influences of White Culture on the Hopi Kachina Cult.* Bulletin 35, Cranbrook Institute of Science, Bloomfield.

1979 "Hopi history, 1850–1940," *Handbook of North American Indians* vol. 9 (Southwest), pp. 524–532, Alfonso Ortiz, volume editor, W. C. Sturtevant, general editor, Smithsonian Institution, Washington, D. C.

Donaldson, Thomas C.
1893 *Eleventh Census of the United States, Robert P. Porter, Superintendent, Extra Census Bulletin, Moqui Pueblo Indians of Arizona and Pueblo Indians of New Mexico.* United States Census Printing Office, Washington, D. C.

Douglas, F. H.
1934 "Symbolism in Indian art and the difficulties of its interpretation," *Denver Art Museum Leaflet* 61, Denver.

Dozier, Edward P.

 1954 "The Hopi-Tewa of Arizona," *University of California Publications in American Archaeology and Ethnology,* vol. 44, no. 3.

 1966 *Hano A Tewa Indian Community in Arizona.* Holt, Rinehart and Winston, New York.

Eggan, Fred

 1934 Letter to John Collier, Commissioner of Indian Affairs 1-11-1934, National Archives, Hopi Files.

 1966 *The American Indian Perspectives for the Study of Social Change.* Aldine, Chicago.

Ellis, Forence H.

 1959 "An Outline of Laguna Pueblo history and social organization," *Southwestern Journal of Anthropology* 15:325–347.

Fergusson, Erna

 1931 *Dancing Gods Indian Ceremonials of New Mexico and Arizona.* Alfred A. Knopf, New York.

Fewkes, Jesse Walter

 1898 "Archaeological expedition to Arizona in 1895," *Seventeenth Annual Report of the Bureau of American Ethnology,* Smithsonian Institution, Government Printing Office, Washington, D. C., reprinted Dover Publications, New York, 1973.

 1899 "The Winter solstice altars at Hano Pueblo," *American* Anthropologist 1.2: 251–276.

 1900 "Tusayan migration traditions," *Nineteenth Annual Report of the Bureau of American Ethnology,* Part 2, Smithsonian Institution, Government Printing Office, Washington, D. C.

 1919 "Designs on prehistoric Hopi pottery," *Thirty-third Annual Report of the Bureau of American Ethnology,* Smithsonian Institution, Government Printing Office, Washington, D. C., reprinted Dover Publications, New York, 1973.

Frank, Larry, and Francis H. Harlow

 1974 *Historic Pottery of the Pueblo Indians: 1600–1880.* New York Graphic Society, Boston.

Frisbie, Theodore R.

 1973 "The Influence of J. Walter Fewkes on Nampayo: fact or fancy?" In *The Changing Ways of Southwestern Indians, A Historical Perspective,* Albert H. Schroeder, ed., Rio Grande Press, Glorieta.

Gill, Robert R.

 1976 "Ceramic arts and acculturation at Laguna," In *Ethnic and Tourist Arts,* Nelson H. H. Graburn, ed., University of California Press, Berkeley.

Haas, Theodore H.

 1947 *Ten Years of Tribal Government Under the I.R.A.* U. S. Department of the Interior, Washington, D. C.

Hail, Barbara A.

 1980 *Hau, Kóla!* Studies in Anthropology and Material Culture, vol. 3, Haffenreffer Museum of Anthropology, Brown University, Providence.

Hammond, Ernest
1934 Letter to John Collier, Commissioner of Indian Affairs, February, National Archives, Hopi Files.

Harlow, Francis H.
1977 *Modern Pueblo Pottery, 1880–1960.* Northland Press, Flagstaff.

Harper, Allen G.
1936 Letter to Alexander G. Hutton, Superintendent, Hopi Agency, National Archives, Hopi Files.

Hitchcock, Ann
1977 "A Consumer's guide to Hopi pottery," *Plateau* 49.3:22–31.

Hough, Walter
1917 "A Revival of the ancient Hopi pottery art," *American Anthropologist* 19: 322–323.
1918 "The Hopi Indian collection in the United States National Museum," *United States National Museum Proceedings* 54:235–296.

Hubert, Virgil
1937 "An Introduction to Hopi pottery design," *Museum Notes* 10.1, Museum of Northern Arizona, Flagstaff.

Indian Law Resource Center
1979 *Report to the Kikmongwis on Document 196 and the Hopi Tribal Council,* Washington, D. C.

James, George W.
1914 *Indian Blankets and Their Makers.* Dover, New York, reprinted 1974.

James, Harry C.
1974 *Pages From Hopi History.* University of Arizona Press, Tucson.

Jennings, Jesse D.
1974 *Prehistory of North America.* (2nd edition) McGraw-Hill, New York.

Keam, Thomas V.
1886 Letter to D. Atkins, Commissioner of Indian Affairs, 1-2-1886, National Archives, Hopi Files.

Kennard, Edward A.
1979 "Hopi economy and subsistence," *Handbook of North American Indians* vol. 9 (Southwest), pp. 554–563, Alfonso Ortiz, volume editor, W. C. Sturtevant, general editor, Smithsonian Institution, Washington, D. C.

Kikmongwi of Shungopavi
1934 Letter to John Collier, 3-4-1934, National Archives, Hopi Files.

La Farge, Oliver
1936 Letter to John Collier, Commissioner of Indian Affairs, 8-28-1936, National Archives, Hopi Files.
1929 *Laughing Boy.* Houghton Mifflin, Cambridge.

McChesney, Lea S.
1982 *Reference Manual for Historic Hopi Ceramics.* Peabody Museum Press, Cambridge.

McNitt, Frank
  1962   The Indian Traders. University of Oklahoma Press, Norman.

Means, Florence C.
  1960   Sunlight on the Hopi Mesas. The Judson Press, Philadelphia.

Melville, Maude
  1927a   Letter to Martha Ann Seaman, 6-24-1927, Collection of Maude Arnold,
          Worcester.
  1927b   Diary, Collection of Maude Arnold, Worcester.

Melville Papers
  n.d.   Clark University Archives, Worcester.

Mera, Harry P.
  1938   The Rain Bird: A Study in Pueblo Design. Laboratory of Anthropology,
          Santa Fe, reprinted 1970, Dover Publications, New York.

Mindeleff, Victor
  1891   "A Study of Pueblo architecture in Tusayan and Cibola," Eighth Annual
          Report of the Bureau of American Ethnology, Smithsonian Institution,
          Washington, D. C.

Narvaez Valverde, Fray José
  1937   "Notes upon Moqui and other recent ones upon New Mexico," In Histori-
          cal Documents Relating to New Mexico, Vizcarja, and Approaches
          Thereto, to 1773, vol 3, C. W. Hackett, ed., Carnegie Institute of Washing-
          ton, pp. 385–387, Washington, D. C.

Nequatewa, Edmund
  1936   Truth of a Hopi. Bulletin 8, Museum of Northern Arizona, Flagstaff, re-
          printed 1967 by Northland Press, Flagstaff.
  1943   "Nampeyo, famous Hopi potter," Plateau 15.3:40–42.

Ortiz, Alfonso
  1969   The Tewa World Space, Time, Being, and Becoming in a Pueblo Society.
          University of Chicago Press, Chicago.

Peck, Herbert
  1968   The Book of Rookwood Pottery. Crown Publishers, New York.

Rozaire, Charles E.
  1977   Indian Basketry of Western North America. Brooke House, Los Angeles.

Salyah, Ethel
  1934   Letter to Maude Melville Arnold, 7-18-1934, Melville Collection, Wesleyan
          University.

Shepard, Anna O.
  1956   Ceramics for the Archaeologist. Carnegie Institute of Washington, Publi-
          cation 609, Washington, D. C.

Sikorski, Kathryn A.
  1968   Modern Hopi Pottery. Utah State University, Monograph Series, 15:2, Salt
          Lake City.

Simmons, Marc
1979   "History of the pueblos since 1821," *Handbook of North American Indians* vol. 9 (Southwest), pp. 206–223, Alfonso Ortiz, volume editor, W. C. Sturtevant, general editor, Smithsonian Institution, Washington, D. C.

Smith, Watson
1952   *Kiva Mural Decorations at Awatovi and Kawaika-a.* Papers of the Peabody Museum of American Archaeology and Ethnology, 37, Cambridge.
1971   *Painted Ceramics of the Western Mound at Awatovi,"* Papers of the Peabody Museum of American Archaeology and Ethnology, 38, Cambridge.

Spencer, Robert F., and Jesse D. Jennings, et al.
1977   *The Native Americans.* Harper and Row, New York.

Spicer, Edward H.
1962   *Cycles of Conquest.* University of Arizona Press, Tucson.

Stands In Timber, John, and Margo Liberty
1967   *Cheyenne Memories.* University of Nebraska Press, Lincoln.

Stanislawski, Michael B.
1969   "Hopi-Tewa pottery making: styles of learning." Paper presented at the thirty-fourth annual meetings of the Society for American Archaeology, Milwaukee, Wisconsin.
1978   "If pots were mortal" In *Explorations in Ethno-archaeology*, Richard A. Gould, ed., University of New Mexico Press, Albuquerque.
1979   "Hopi-Tewa," *Handbook of North American Indians* vol. 9 (Southwest), pp. 587–602, Alfonso Ortiz, volume editor, W. C. Sturtevant, general editor, Smithsonian Institution, Washington, D. C.

Stanislawski, Michael B., Barbara B. Stanislawski, and Ann Hitchcock
1976   "Identification marks on Hopi and Hopi-Tewa pottery." *Plateau* 48.3:47– 65.

Stephen, Alexander M.
1936   *Hopi Journal of Alexander M. Stephen* (2 vols.), Elsie Clews Parsons, ed., Columbia University Contributions to Anthropology 23, New York.

Stevenson, James
1883   "Illustrated Catalogue of the collections obtained from the Indians of New Mexico and Arizona," *Second Annual Report of the Bureau of American Ethnology*, Smithsonian Institution, Government Printing Office, Washington, D. C.

Titiev, Mischa
1944   *Old Oraibi: A Study of the Hopi Indians of Third Mesa.* Papers of the Peabody Museum of American Archaeology and Ethnology 22.1, Cambridge, reprinted 1971, Kraus, New York.

Wade, Edwin L.
1976   *The History of the Southwest Indian Ethnic Art Market.* Ph.D. dissertation, University of Washington, University Microfilms, Ann Arbor.

Wade, Edwin L., and Lea S. McChesney
1980   *America's Great Lost Expedition: The Thomas Keam Collection of Hopi Pottery from the Second Hemenway Expedition, 1890–1894.* The Heard Museum, Phoenix.

1981   *Historic Hopi Ceramics The Thomas V. Keam Collection of the Peabody Museum of Archaeology and Ethnology Harvard University*, Peabody Museum Press, Cambridge.

Walker, Willard
    1974   "Palowahtiwa and the economic redevelopment of Zuni Pueblo," *Ethnohistory* 21.1:65–75.

White, A. C.
    1929a   Letter to Mrs. Carey E. Melville, 5-29-1929, Melville Collection, Wesleyan University.
    1929b   Letter to Mrs. Carey E. Melville, 5-30-1929, Melville Collection, Wesleyan University.

Wright, Barton, with illustrations by Cliff Bahnimptewa
    1973   *Kachinas: A Hopi Artist's Documentary*. Northland Press with the Heard Museum, Flagstaff.

Wyckoff, Lydia L.
    1979   "What makes a Zuni pot a Zuni pot?" Paper presented at the nineteenth annual meetings of the Northeastern Anthropological Association, Henniker, N. H.
    n.d.   "Third Mesa Hopi ceramics: a study of the ceramic domain," MS.